Seven Steps to the
Top of the Mountain

Life Is Full of Choices Series

life is full of choices

John Emra

www.LifeIsFullOfChoices.org

Creative
Team
Publishing

Creative Team Publishing
San Diego

© 2011 by John Emra.

Permissions and Credits:

Hand drawn ambigram "Choice/Destiny" by Mark Palmer, owner/artist Red Chapter Clothing, a premium line of clothing and accessories based entirely on his unique ambigram artwork, is used by permission

Quote from Dan Wagner, Senior Homicide Prosecutor, Orange County, California, is used by permission.

ISBN: 978-0-9838919-2-5
PUBLISHED BY CREATIVE TEAM PUBLISHING
www.CreativeTeamPublishing.com
San Diego

Printed in the United States of America

Seven Steps to the
Top of the Mountain

Life Is Full of Choices Series

life is full of choices

John Emra

www.LifeIsFullOfChoices.org

There are three types of parents:

- Those who make things happen with their kids
- Those who watch things happen with their kids
- Those who ask, "What is happening with my kids?"

This book is dedicated to those who choose to move from wondering and watching to becoming those who make things happen with their kids.

.

The Three Cornerstones

Cornerstone Number One — Empowerment
Life is full of choices,
and the choices I make today
will determine the qualities of my life
both now and in the future.

Cornerstone Number Two — Responsibility
Life is full of choices,
and the choices I make today
can affect the circumstances of my life
and other people's lives
both now and in the future.

Cornerstone Number Three — Freedom
Life is full of choices,
and even though I have not chosen
all the circumstances of my life,
I alone determine its qualities, because
life is full of choices,
and the choices I make today
will determine the qualities of my life
both now and in the future.

The Four Core Needs

Affection
Anything we do to make a child feel good
about him or herself.

Boundaries
The pre-arranged limits that are placed on behavior.

Consistency
Doing what you said you would do.

Discipline
The actions that are taken to instill in a child
the understanding of right and wrong
in order to shape their character
so they learn how to make healthy choices.

Table of Contents

Parenting Is Not Easy

As a parent, sometimes it is nice to get help. But you already knew that. That's why you are reading a parenting book. Reading it will not make parenting easy. However, practicing the steps you find here can make parenting easier.

The first thing you need to know is that this book is written for the benefit of everyone who will be parenting your kids. I will spend time in the final sections talking about two people who must speak with one voice, but here at the beginning I am addressing the people who actually compose the group that will help raise your kids. I want to teach all of them how to work through this book.

I have kids, and one thing I discovered early on was that it is almost impossible to raise kids alone. As I am writing words and suggesting activities, I am envisioning a husband and wife working on these things together: two people sitting at a table or on a bench somewhere communicating and cooperating with each other for the benefit of their kids.

If this is not your situation, it's okay. The information contained within this book, including the steps that will help you get to the top of the mountain, will be helpful to the reader. So, read on.

In our world there may be lots of reasons why your parenting group does not start with, or include, a husband and wife. Frankly, the reasons do not matter. Your situation is what it is and you and your support group are raising your kids. Grandparents can partner with a single parent. Extended family and friends can have a part, too. At the very least you may require day care or the assistance of a babysitter.

The bottom line is that the people who are going to be involved in raising a child should cooperate. One way to do that is to work through this book together. Kids operate better within a consistent environment. If everyone obeys the same instructions then the whole group has a better chance of working together and cooperating because they are on the same page.

Your journey into learning the skills of parenting can include partnering with other like-minded people. Create a cooperative effort between your family and another family with a similar outlook on raising kids. This additional family should be composed of individuals you can feel comfortable with, that you trust. Going through this book with them would be most advantageous.

Partnering does not mean all the participants have to be sitting in the same room while reading the book together. It means that if this week both families are working on Step

One, your cooperative venture gives you other people you can share your ideas with. Even if they are not at the same point in this process, you can still talk about how you are doing and be encouraged with the knowledge that you and your spouse are not alone in this journey of raising your kids. You can meet together and act as a support group for each other.

A partner can be a person on your block or a sibling across town. Partnering can be done in a small group at church or with someone you see at work. It's mutually helpful. Partnering also might include people on different stages of the journey of parenting, where one is further ahead than another. Partners can still work together in much the same way a coach works with a team. Partnering gives all the participants someone to talk with and be encouraged by, and it gives you a chance to establish again what you are doing with your kids.

Your story is your own, of course. As you go through this book and grow through your experiences you may want to share your success with others. That is why at the end of each chapter you will find blank pages you can use as a journal, to keep a record of what is working, how your kids are reacting, and suggestions you may have for other people. It is good to look around you and find people who are involved in some aspect of parenting outside your own partnering circle, and share your story with them.

Your stories will encourage others and give them ideas they might not have thought of on their own. You will also be encouraged by the stories of others.

As a parent have you:
- Lost your temper?
- Run out of answers?
- Become so frustrated you just wanted to scream at them or at yourself?
- Noticed that parenting situations and styles are causing problems between you and your spouse?

All of these are symptoms of a phenomenon I call parenting in the valley.

Most parents will tell you that discipline issues are at the heart of the serious problems when it comes to raising children. For instance:
- How should I discipline my kids?
- What actually should I say or do at the moment?
- Should I _____ or _____ when they misbehave?
- How can I make them mind me?
- Should I even try to make them mind me?
- How strict should I be?
- When should I show grace?
- How do I make the rules?
- What rules should I enforce?

All of these are good questions and some are difficult to answer for a variety of reasons. It is those reasons that make parenting and disciplining kids so difficult. The bad news is I will not be able to answer those specific questions for you or any of the hundreds of questions you may come up with, because this book is not designed to answer them. The good news is this book will walk you, step by step, through the process of creating a system within which you can answer those questions for yourself, while at the same time teaching you how to make a difference in the patterns you establish or have already established for disciplining your kids. This book will show you in seven steps how to parent from the mountaintop.

Let's make sure we understand what I mean by parenting from the mountaintop. I hope you are reading this book because you have already read the companion book *Parenting From the Top of the Mountain,* and you want to incorporate into your life the strategies found there.

The first book in the *Life Is Full of Choices Series, Cornerstones and Core Needs of Growing Kids* presents the foundation. The second book in the series, *Parenting From the Top of the Mountain* takes the lessons and skills of the first book and applies them to the job of parenting. This book, *Seven Steps to the Top of the Mountain* is written as a step by step guide to make it easier for parents to incorporate the Four Core Needs and the Three Cornerstones into their lives and the lives of their children.

It is possible for you to understand the concepts by reading only the parenting books, but reading *Cornerstones and Core Needs of Growing Kids* will give you a more complete understanding of the concepts we present. *Cornerstones and Core Needs of Growing Kids* sets the foundation. As you read *Parenting From the Top of the Mountain* you will be able to build the framework for more effective parenting. *Seven Steps to the Top of the Mountain* guides you through the seven finishing steps. It will be easier to implement the lessons here when you read the preceding two books.

If you have already read *Parenting From the Top of the Mountain* let me reiterate that the top of the mountain is not a place of superiority. It is not a place where you can rule over your household and your kids. It is not a position of power where you can look down on your subjects and control them. In fact you will see that the top of the mountain is not a place at all. The top of the mountain is a state of mind.

Getting into the proper frame of mind, however, may require finding a physical place where you and your spouse can enter a mutual mindset of parenting, a location free of distraction where you can both focus on what's really important. This place should be one of peace and relaxation for you. Finding it and setting aside a time to dwell there are essential to thinking and reflecting together without the pressures of the day or the needs of tomorrow invading and dominating your thoughts.

You may find your mountaintop on your couch, on the porch swing after the kids go to bed or at the kitchen table enjoying a cup of tea while they are taking a nap. I talked with one couple and found out that their top of the mountain was their hot tub. It may be that getting up early together and spending the time over breakfast works for you. I know a husband who has to go to work early in the morning so he gets up and fixes breakfast for himself and his wife, then serves it to her in bed while they visit on the mountaintop. You may need to schedule a babysitter and get away, or let the grandparents take care of the kids. Whatever you need to do to find your magical place of peace, do it.

Email conversations, texting, and social network chatter just won't work for this exercise. The purpose is in-person communication, not just the sharing of words. Be in the same place at the same time, physically and mentally, to work through the parenting issues you must deal with.

If one person is distracted, the mountaintop experience won't work. It doesn't matter what interrupts you, distractions of any kind limit the time well spent on the top of the mountain. You may need to spend the time talking about issues other than those of your kids before you can deal with the issues concerning your kids. I don't know what your situation is, but again, do what needs to be done so you can go to your mountaintop and find peace there — free of interruptions and needless diversions.

Most parents don't go to their mountaintop often enough. Some parents or partners don't even know there is such a place or how to find it, because children keep them busy, life is fast, and noise is everywhere. In fact, sometimes when a parents get a moment of peace and quiet they don't want to share it with anyone, not even their spouse. Those factors and others like them contribute to a state of mind that can be best described as chaotic on normal days and close to insane on bad ones.

Make the hard choices of parenting on the mountaintop where you are insulated from the pressures of daily living. Making the tough choices there liberates you from making hurried and sometimes regrettable choices in the middle of the emotional struggles found in the valley.

When you are parenting from the mountaintop, you will want to find ways to get your kids up there with you. When kids are small they will sit on your shoulders and you can point out landmarks and danger signs that are visible on the horizon. They will enjoy the view even though they won't fully understand the purpose of being there or the meaning of what they are seeing. If you are consistent in taking them with you to "see the sights," they will understand more as they grow. The rewards of your time on the top of the mountain with them will begin to pay off.

There is a huge contrast between the clarity of the mountaintop and the confusion of the valley. I have hiked through many valleys. When I trudge through the valley it is always hard to tell where I am in relation to the landmarks. Without a compass or a well marked trail, moments of uncertainty are sure to crop up. When I make the effort to get up higher, however, I can see where I want to go and even have an idea of how to get there.

Things look and feel differently when I am struggling to get through tangled thorn bushes, poison oak, and the poison ivy of the valley. With the uncertainty of not knowing exactly where I am, I have to find ways to get around the thick underbrush and ford the raging streams. Plus, I have to do all of this as trees block my view of the landmarks I may have picked if I plotted my course in advance.

Many parents come to the job of parenting with this mindset, "What I have to do is keep going and eventually I will get somewhere and that may be just as good as it gets." They might see other parents or partners who seem to know where they are going but never quite figure out how to get the help they need to be part of that group. They are stuck in the valley.

In the valley it is hard to tell how I arrived there, where I am going, or how to get out. I might know where I want to end up, but I don't know if I should turn a little more to the right, or a little to the left, or just go straight ahead in order to arrive at the destination I want. I may not be completely lost, but I'm not always sure where I am. Not knowing where I am and not being sure of the way can be disconcerting in the valley where forests impede views and underbrush clogs paths. This condition can be unnerving to parents and demoralizing to the role of parenting.

The result of this condition is devastating in the lives of those kids who are living it.

Wouldn't it be nice if someone invented a parenting GPS to keep us on track? As parents or partners we look for signs that reassure us we are going in the right direction. We want advance warnings like, "Curves! Bumps! Bridge Out! Dangers Ahead!" We would like to know where the next rest stop is located or the next view point so we can take a breather and see our way forward. As parents we want to know that we are doing well — we want to know we are on the right path to raise our kids.

This book will take the truths of *Parenting From the Top of the Mountain* and, in seven steps, show how you can incorporate them into your life and parenting. Following these steps will make the process of parenting easier for you and more enjoyable for your kids. Your chances of success will be greatly improved, plus you will learn how to track your successes, celebrate your victories, and share your positive results with others who want to learn, too.

Use the steps. Embrace the process. Enjoy your kids.

1
Step One: Go to the Top of the Mountain

Find your quiet spot.

It sounds so easy. It is not — especially if you already have kids.

Before the kids arrived you could take the time to find a quiet spot to contemplate what should be your course of action, how you want to react and what you will say at any given moment.

Then, the day after your first child enters the scene many of those carefully thought-out plans go right out the window. Your child is not cooperating.

I saw a poster in the home of a couple with two kids. It said: "Once I had no children and a plan for how to raise them. Now I have two children and no plan." If you can relate to that poster, you are not alone.

When you have kids your life becomes a matter of survival. It is a struggle to get enough sleep, to fix meals, do the laundry. Ten minutes to take a shower is considered a luxury.

With kids comes responsibility like you have never felt before. You have to take care of that child's needs. It doesn't matter what else is going on in your world. When a diaper needs to be changed, your child will make sure you know that it must be changed *now*. When Junior is hungry, he will not quit voicing his opinion until he is fed. When he has had enough sleep, even if it is two in the morning, he wants to get up and play and he wants it to happen right then.

Your life no longer is yours. You are no longer free to do with it what you want. Your choice to have a child means that your life has become focused on meeting the needs of another person.

Having a baby sounds like a fun thing to do. Many teenage girls talk about having a baby so they'll have someone who will love them. But they are not being told, or they are not listening when someone tells them, that the six or eight months of getting up every three or four hours to feed that baby takes its toll on their sanity and wellbeing. No one tells them that the love they so desperately want doesn't happen until after a lot of hard work happens first, and in some cases, it never happens at all.

Parenting is not like signing up and playing Little League where you can quit if you don't like it. Parenting is the most difficult life-changing experience you will ever have and it starts with a little bundle of joy that only cares about him or herself.

The result is fatigue, and every good manual for leadership will tell you that fatigue is the number one cause of poor judgment.

In parenting, when fatigue results in poor judgment, kids can get hurt. We can yell at them. We may say mean things that we wouldn't say to a neighbor or friend. We might use a tone of voice that can scar their psyche for the rest of their life. Kids can get spanked, hit, shaken, or worse because of our frustration that very often is the result of fatigue.

I applaud your effort to seek out help so that you don't parent in these negative ways. If you don't get anything else out of reading this book, please understand the need that parents have to get enough rest. This is critical for your health and the wellbeing of your kids.

So your question now is, "How *can* I get enough rest? You have already said how difficult being a parent is and that the first few months are a struggle to survive." My answer is, I don't know your situation, your resources, and how must rest you require. I can make some practical suggestions, though. You will have to make your own choices as to how to get the rest you need. Here are some ideas to consider:

- If you have one child, take a nap every time they do. Forget about the dishes and the laundry—just take the nap—you need it.
- If you don't need the rest now, you will need it tonight.

"That's great advice, but I have two children and their naps aren't always synchronized, so now what do I do?"

- Take every opportunity to take a nap whenever they both go down. I know that will seldom happen but work toward timing their feeding schedule so they may go down at the same time. Have a neighbor come over to take care of your kids today while you take a nap and tomorrow go to her house so she can take a nap.
- As soon as your husband comes in the door give him a kiss and hand him the kids for an hour or two so you can take a nap. When he says, "Wait a minute! I have been working all day, I'm tired, and need some down time," just look at him and sweetly say, "I will trade you responsibilities any day you would like."

- Are grandparents close enough so they can spend the night once in a while and give you a whole night of sleep? Maybe they can spend the day so you can take a nap.

My brother and his wife had a set of twins as their first children. After a short time they were both exhausted. They were doing everything they could do to get the rest they needed, but with twins it seemed that if one child was crying they both were crying; if one had a need they both had it. They would just get one to sleep and the other would wake up and start crying and remember that when one was crying they both would cry, so both cried.

My parents started going to their house and spending one night every weekend. There were bottles to fix, diapers to change, babies to rock, some laundry to do, and a few dishes in the sink. They were busy all night long, but my brother and his wife were able to sleep because someone else was responsible for the kids. That one night helped them get through the rest of the week.

All this information about how hard it is to rest, and how important it is to get enough rest, is to get us started on the topic of *realizing the importance of finding your mountaintop, your place of peace and quiet.*

Once you have discovered your top of the mountain,

find where and when you and your spouse can share some mountaintop time there. For some people the mountaintop might be their kitchen table. For others it might be Starbucks. If I lived in Spokane, Washington, it would be the Rocket Bakery. They have the best oatmeal bars I have ever tasted.

The reason you and your spouse need to meet together is because parenting is a group activity. I know there are single parents who, either because of their choices or because their circumstances have changed, are raising kids on their own. The solutions that we are talking about apply to single parents as well as couples. When I refer to parents or a spouse you just need to insert the proper term or title that fits your situation.

Whether you are on your own or part of a larger group, the truth is still that parenting is a group activity. Whoever is raising the kids must find the time and the space in which they can deal with the issues that have come up and those that are coming up. Some of the issues you should consider at the top of the mountain:

- Agree what you are gong to feed the little darlings.
- If you are going to work toward setting a schedule for feeding and bed time make those choices now.
- Divide up the responsibilities now so you are not fighting at 2:00 AM about whose turn it is to get up with Jr.
- Eventually there will be discipline issues to discuss

and rules to establish. Start when they are infants. Establish a pattern that you and your spouse or parenting partners can follow when the kids are bigger and the issues larger and more difficult to resolve.

One problem my wife and I had in our early parenting years was that our schedules weren't often in synch. She is a morning person and does her best contemplative thinking in the morning. I on the other hand get out of bed ready to work on my list in the morning. I am pretty task oriented and can't sit and relax until everything on my list is taken care of. I contemplate events or situations better in the evening.

It took us quite a while to realize the solution for us was for me to write, "Have some quiet time with Sheryl" on my list; I could choose to get up in the morning, sit and process with her about how to deal with this situation, or plan what we wanted to do if another situation occurred. That was the solution that worked for us. Regardless of the solution you choose, both parents and all caregivers need to be on the same page when it comes to dealing with kids.

Multiple studies have shown the three biggest issues that lead to divorce are money, sex, and kids. I am not going to talk about money or sex, but finding and using your mountaintop can help with the issue of kids, and spending time together talking about the kids might help with at least one of the other issues.

We will talk about the importance of consistency later. But for now understand that if I reacted one way and Sheryl reacted a different way when our sons would do something wrong, we would at best be fuming in silence that the other parent was not doing it right and at worst we would be fighting in front of the kids over how the other one should have done it.

It doesn't matter what *it* was. We just needed to be in agreement on the best way to handle *it*. Sheryl and I needed to sit down in a quiet place at a quiet time and carefully and thoroughly discuss the issues so that when *it* happened we already had an answer to the question "what do I do?" We reached agreement by talking on the mountaintop. Considering the issues in advance that might cause emotional problems helped us be consistent when we were physically in the valley with our kids. As a couple we would work through every possible scenario we could think of. There was no correct place or time. Place and time are the best for you when they work for you.

If you need some background music, fine. If you need a candle or lights bright enough to read by, that is fine, too. You can sit at the table or in easy chairs in the living room. You can be at home or in the park. The possibilities are endless. The only thing that matters is this: find a time and a place where you can communicate with your spouse.

It doesn't matter how often you meet. You meet for this purpose when you need to meet. At the beginning you may want to meet every day. After you have worked some things out you may only need to meet once every few days and eventually once a week.

It also doesn't matter who is leading this conversation. It probably is best for the person to take the lead who has something to say. A good way to start is, "I'm having a problem with Billy."

"Okay, what is the problem?"

"He is not respecting my authority. When I tell him to clear his dishes from the table after his lunch he rolls his eyes and heaves a big sigh. His reaction bothers me."

"Okay, so what is the rule?"

"The rule is he needs to 'respect others.'"

"And what is the consequence we chose to use when he does not respect someone else?"

"...that he would go to timeout for five minutes."

"Have you been doing that?"

"No. It just seems like such a small thing to get upset about."

"How long has this been going on?"

"About two weeks."

"What has happened during the last two weeks when you have done nothing?"

"It has gotten worse."

"So what do you think will happen if you continue to do nothing?"

"It will continue to get worse and eventually I will get frustrated and blow up at him."

"So what should we do?"

"I guess I need to follow though on the consequence we had established."

"Okay, so how does that feel?"

"It helps knowing I have a plan."

"Okay, so what else is going on?

I have never had this exact conversation with my wife, but I have participated in hundreds just like it and listened to lots of couples describing the need to have this conversation.

There are two things worth noting in this scenario. One is the total lack of emotion. We were discussing a factual event or in another instance something that might become a factual event. We were not pointing fingers and saying if you had done what we talked about then this would or would not have occurred.

We were discussing a situation and agreeing that a certain plan of action was needed to remedy the situation. We were agreeing that when a situation arose we would do a certain action so that the problem would not continue to get bigger. We projected the result to be that our son would learn to respect authority. And we knew we should fix the problem while it remained small. If we chose to wait, we knew that someday he would be standing before a judge, and while the result would be a "time out", it would be an extended one, certainly harder on everyone than going to his room for five minutes.

The second thing worth noticing in the exchange is that the solution had already been chosen. At a prior time we had already talked about respecting authority and what the result of stepping over that boundary would look like. In this discussion the solution came after we had said, "What should *we* do?" Not "This is what *you* need to do..." or "Why aren't you doing what we have already talked about?"

In the exchange I was not pointing fingers and trying to figure out when and how my spouse screwed up. If that is where we were going there would not be many more times of sitting down and talking about it. Husbands don't enjoy being yelled at. Neither do wives. If we started yelling at each other then we would not be on top on the mountain anymore. Peace would have left the building and contentment would not be far behind. We would have to find a way to get back to the top of the mountain where we could chart the course anew and start working on the issues children are producing in *our* lives.

In the scenario you just read we were a team and we were committed to working on this together. Was it easy to stay calm and detached at a moment like this? No. It was especially hard if we had revisited the same problem two or three times in the same week.

Could I talk about how frustrated I was that we were dealing with this same topic *again*? Yes, I could express that frustration but I also needed to do it in a calm manner and with a quiet, loving voice.

You may be asking, "What? How do you expect me to do *that*?!"

Settle down. It looks impossible but it is not. It is not what our culture is good at teaching us to do, so it appears hard to do at first. Once a pattern is established it does get easier.

You will be glad that you set up a pattern of behavior in advance when you talk about your choice to stop at Burger King on the way home from the mall even though there was already an agreement not to do fast food between meals. At that moment your spouse may want to get upset and yell, proclaiming that this is the third time, and what is the use of having our agreements if you are not going to do what you had already talked about, anyway...

As you can see this process works both ways. There will be times when you will feel the urge to yell at your spouse, and most assuredly your spouse will have those same feelings. Working in advance to have agreements in place and adhering to them is harder to abide by if the behavior pattern you have lived with has been focused on finding out who is to blame or blowing up at each other. Advance planning and agreement is a new system for many, but it does work if a couple sticks to the rules.

In our parenting illustration, one of the big rules we followed was this: instead of trying to figure out who was wrong, deal with Billy's behavior in light of prior agreements. In the absence of a prior agreement, find something we have agreed upon that comes close so we can start there in order to solve this issue.

So how does a parenting couple, or people who are partnering with parents, begin? The very first time you sit down on the top of your mountain you need to establish several parameters of engagement.

First, create the boundaries within which your kids can operate and identify how you are going to reward the kids for operating within them. Then identify the results of choices that cross over those boundaries.

I said it that way on purpose. Find the boundary and set the reward, first. We spend so much time handing out the consequence for crossing a boundary that sometimes we forget that there are positive consequences, too. Focus more energy looking for what we can reward.

I prefer general boundaries and I think that a few of them is better than many. My favorites are:
- Respect God.
- Respect yourself.
- Respect others.
- Respect the stuff.

Use these if you would like, or create others that work better for you.

Once you have defined the general boundaries, start identifying specific choices and their consequences. If one behavior not allowed in the house is throwing the toys, then figure out the consequence of that wrong behavior. Throwing a toy is not respecting the stuff (the house or the toy) and if the kid throws it at anyone then they're not respecting the other person.

If you choose there will be no swearing because that is not respecting God or others, then choose the consequence for that misdeed. This consequence can be different than the one for throwing the toy or it can be the same. What the consequence is may not be as important as you think. The issue is not finding the right consequence; it is about finding one that will work *for you, your spouse, and your parenting partners.* When the consequence is chosen write it down so you remember and the kids will know.

Spend time choosing ten or fifteen behaviors that you and your spouse want to encourage. These can include sharing, saying "please" or "thank you," and picking up the toys without being asked. Then discover an equal number of behaviors that you are not going to allow and then choose the consequence. The goal is to identify as many behaviors that deserve positive consequences as those that warrant negative consequences.

The overall purpose is to apply the Three Cornerstones of Life Is Full of Choices in the lives of our kids. They need to discover that their choices have consequences, good choices produce good results and poor choices produce negative results. Once they experience this truth they quickly learn it is their choice to live within the boundaries or to cross them. The choice of positive or negative consequences is their choice to make. Either way the results are known in advance.

What I like about these general boundaries is that they provide a solid framework within which you can reward your kids, and at the same time they cover just about everything a kid could get in trouble for. You can get specific and list twenty or even fifty, but you will never cover everything. Kids will always find a way to surprise you. That is why I prefer the general rather than the specific boundaries.

Once you have the boundaries, the consequences you choose are totally up to you. Consequences for a two year old will be different from those for a ten year old. The expectations of how those boundaries play out will also be unique to the age of the child.

A two year old with a defiant attitude saying "No!" is different than a ten year old with the same attitude saying the same thing. As the age dictates levels of understanding so consequences should match those levels.

The two year old might receive a form of appropriate discipline that could include a couple minutes of time out or the temporary loss of a special toy. The ten year old could be grounded for the rest of the day, get an added job after dinner or get his "screen time" taken away. At that age, going without TV, computer, and video games will often get his attention faster than anything else.

You do not need to choose what to do in every situation where some form of correction is needed – there are too many. You should, however, look for what might be the first signs of a problem as they start to emerge. For example, if you can detect the early stages of "not respecting other people" you can react when the transgression is small and prevent it from growing larger and becoming serious.

A little correction in the beginning before a problem gets out of hand can often teach a good lesson without major ramifications. And if kids are taught what respect for others looks like when they are two, there will not need to be so much teaching later when they are ten.

Kids will still push the line, just to make sure you are paying attention, but overall it will be easier. There is that word I promised you, *easier.*

Parenting gets easier when planned from the mountaintop. It may have been time consuming to get started but the benefit for you is that the time spent early will pay dividends later in life when things go smoother.

After setting boundaries and consequences for bad

behaviors, parents must find ways of continually positively reinforcing their kids when they react within the boundary. I can hear it now because I've heard it before over and over again. "Why should I reward them for doing what they should be doing in the first place?" "They should do what is right just because I said so."

That's true. The problem is: they don't necessarily know how. Parents need to teach them how to do what they need to do. Succeeding in this world requires knowing how to treat other people. Parents must teach them how to share, converse, disagree without disrespecting, and how to comply. They will need all of those skills in order to go to school, make friends, and eventually hold down a job. Another benefit: they need those skills in order to grow up and live on their own. Without those skills they'll be forced to live in your second bedroom for the rest of your life.

Rewards come to everyone for doing things that we should do anyway. When we pay our bills on time we get a better credit rating. When we pay in advance we sometimes get a discount on the interest rate. When we do our job well we get a promotion. If we show up to work on time we get a paycheck. Rewarding good behavior is the way the world works. We should use it as we work with our kids.

One important fact here: you might have noticed that the boundaries are all positive in nature, instructing what to do as opposed to instructing what not to do. If all we do is tell them what not to do their attention is continually focused on the negative. All they know is where not to go, so that is the place they end up going.

Start with the positive. Begin by explaining what we want our kids *to do* and what the reward will be for doing it. When we do this we face them in the direction we want them to go.

As a parent, if I am more focused on what I want them to do then I become more conscious of the times when they are doing what I want them to do. I reward the behaviors I want to encourage. When they wander or purposefully go the other direction, which they will do, it is *easier* to turn them back the way they were facing than it is to turn them in a direction they have never been before.

Cornerstones and Core Needs of Growing Kids emphasized that kids need boundaries, and that they need us as parents to be consistent in the application of those boundaries. But my mother use to say that you can catch a whole lot more bees with honey than you can with vinegar.

One philosophy is that you need to have at least three positive consequences for every negative one. That may be true. This I know: if I consistently apply negative consequences when someone infringes on a boundary, my children will *learn* not to go there. If I am consistent with giving positive consequences when they are staying within a boundary, they *want* to go there.

Let's conclude that you have established the boundaries and have both positive and negative consequences in place to deal with what might be the first tests you will see. If you are paying attention, you'll see them.

If your kids are old enough to have a conversation about boundaries and consequences then explain how this all works. You will know they are old enough when they start interacting with you by saying "No!" When *no* becomes their new favorite word, an explanation is in order.

Be careful. Your consistency is on the line here. If you say it, be ready to do it. Choose your boundaries and consequences carefully. Be very careful with the words you use. Explain yourself fully in language and expressions they understand and then ask questions to make sure you have been understood.

Give them examples and tell them what will happen when boundaries are crossed or honored. Then give them more examples and ask them to tell you what will happen.

What we want is clarity. Clarity of understanding means communication has taken place.

For older kids you might use a written contract. Again,

be careful because a contract is a commitment between two parties. You can hold them to their part of the contract, but remember, they *will* hold you to your part, too.

At this point you have done a lot of mental and emotional work. If the kids don't get the picture it is going to be difficult when they start whining that you didn't tell them. There will be whining anyway but it will be the whining that says, "Oh, I didn't think you were serious." Your consistency proves you were.

When the kids know you are serious they will try to wear you down, divide the parenting team, and find out how they can use this new system to their advantage. That is all the more reason your main job description needs to be focused on growing and maintaining consistency.

Step One Action:

- Work with your spouse to find a good top of the mountain place and time that works for both of you.
  - o Individually make a list of the possibilities, and then compare lists.
  - o Provide other items needed, i.e. coffee, tea, candles, music...

    You will know you are successful and that you have reached the top of the mountain when *together* you shared that relaxed feeling of "Ah."

- Visit your Top of the Mountain on a regular basis. Use that time and place to make discipline decisions apart from the pressures of daily life. Start small so you can be successful in numerous ways.
  - o Go slowly. Stay relaxed.
  - o Work together on communication so you both are in agreement.
  - o Keep a list of what you are agreeing to. If you want, you can use the following pages in this book to keep your thoughts together.

  You will know you are successful when you can't wait to talk to each other the next time. You will want to share *both* what is working and what isn't working without condemnation or criticism.

- Meet with your kids to explain that things are going to change and what life will look like when the changes occur.
  - o Start with an apology for what you haven't been doing.
  - o Don't bombard them with 50 things right off the bat. Start slowly with them, too.
  - o Encourage them to ask questions but don't force it. This is new for them just as it was for you.

  You will know you are succeeding when things get worse. Kids like consistency and you are changing things. Of course it is going to get worse. These times provide more opportunities to practice your consistency.

- Consistency is not easy. Both parents must work on being consistent with each other on the issues you both face. Begin by working on your personal consistency day after day.
    - o I need to be consistent with myself day after day.
    - o I need to be consistent with what my spouse does.
    - o We need to be consistent with all our kids.

    You will know you have achieved success when your kids stop going from one parent to the other one with the hope of getting a better answer.
- As you see things change, make some notes in your journal. Use these notes to encourage yourselves and others that what you are doing is working. Two pages are provided after each step for keeping this journal.
- Though you may not see big changes right away, stay focused on the little victories and be encouraged with the little things.

Journaling Pages for Step One

The notes you make in your journal will help you remember your story. When people ask what is happening, or what is working, your journal will bring to mind things you may have forgotten. Your story from this step, about why you chose to parent from the top of the mountain and how it has gone in the beginning, will be helpful to others who are just starting. They will especially be interested in hearing the answers to these questions:

- Where is your mountaintop?
- What boundaries are you choosing?
- How have those boundaries been tested by your kids?
- What are the positive consequences and negative consequences that are associated with those boundaries?
- How have your kids reacted to the changes you have instigated?

Journaling Pages for Step One

Journaling Pages for Step One

2
Step Two: Choose What You Want to Teach

You've heard the phrase, "our place in the greater scheme of things." Finding "our place" is a life-long journey. If you're a parent you know that parenting occupies a central place in the greater scheme of rearing up a child. Parenting includes instruction, of course, and the bottom line is this: *what* we teach our kids really matters.

A discussion about "greater scheme" often includes this question: do we *determine* our destiny by the choices we make or is our destiny *already determined* and our choices only take us in the directions where destiny awaits?

I recently saw an ambigram on a t-shirt that I fell in love

with and I think it illustrates both sides of this discussion. An ambigram can be a collection of letters that spell the same thing whether it is viewed right side up or upside down. The ambigram I saw is made up of letters that reveal different things depending on your perspective.

I talked to the artist, Mark Palmer, and he gave me permission to use his artwork to illustrate the importance of this point.

If I look at it from one side I can see the word *choice*. If I look at it after turning it, I see *destiny*.

The truth that is apparent within Life Is Full of Choices is that our destiny and our choices are intertwined. This ambigram illustrates that *it is our perspective that determines if our choices make up our destiny or our destiny decides our choices.*

Sometimes we are so committed to our perspective we don't realize there may be other perspectives to consider.

Teaching your kids is all about helping them see the truth of choices and destiny. If you teach them not to worry about studying for that big test, to not bother to plan what they will do with their lives, then you are instilling in them the belief that their destiny is decided and there is nothing they can do about it.

On the other hand if you spend time encouraging them to concentrate on their homework to get the best grades they can, and at a young age you encourage them to think about what they enjoy doing like riding in a fire truck or teaching a class of kids, then you are instilling the belief in them that their choices do matter when it comes to forming their destiny.

I believe we have a great deal of influence on our destiny. Does that mean I am in control of it? No, because other people can affect the circumstances of my life.

If I believe my destiny is to be a grade school teacher, I need to choose to go to school, study, take education courses and eventually graduate and get a Teacher's Certificate. Then I can fulfill the destiny I have created for myself.

Along the way, there are many things that could happen to change where I end up. I could choose to change my emphasis and become a businessman instead of a teacher. I could develop throat cancer and lose my voice. I could even be involved in a car accident and lose my life. Many things could happen on the way to fulfilling what I perceive as my destiny, but if I never go to school and get a degree I will certainly never stand in front of a classroom of eager kids and see the joy on their faces as they learn from me about life.

My choice to instruct others on the importance making choices and seeing consequences has resulted in changed lives. This belief and its outcome have changed my life.

When I was a child someone said to me "In life, aim for the stars. If you don't make it you may end up hitting the moon. But if you aim for the moon you may end up not going anywhere." It is my hope that as parents we would all teach our kids that they can aim for the stars. That is a choice we can make.

Begin with an exercise that will help you and your spouse parent from the mountaintop. This exercise will help you define what is important to you, what you believe in, and what you will teach your kids. In order for this exercise to be most efficient, work together. Working together includes your partners, as well.

Use the numbered spaces beginning on the next page or take a piece of paper and make a list of what you as a couple value. Just write down what comes to mind. In a few minutes you should be able to compile a list of twenty or thirty things.

By "things" I don't necessarily mean physical items. What you value can be a concept. For example: if you value your car that should be on the list, and if you value integrity that also should be on the list.

This list is very important. So, we invite you to stop reading right here, and make your list. Use as many separate sheets of paper as needed.

1 _____

2 _____

3 _____

4 _____

5 _____

6 _____

7 _____

8 _____

9 _____

10 _____

11 _____

12 _____

13 _____

14 _____

15 _____

16 _____

17 _____

18 _____

19 _____

20 _____

Now that you have your list, please divide it into two categories. One category we will call *qualities*, and the other, *circumstances*. The differences between a quality and a circumstance are these: A quality cannot be given to you or taken away from you. You choose a quality. A circumstance happens to you, it can affect you only if you permit it to, and it can be taken away from you.

Take your list and categorize your items.

I did this exercise recently in a parenting class and our group had a problem categorizing "wisdom." Most thought it was a quality. I was not so sure. Eventually it ended up under a circumstance because in life there are people who lose their capacity to think and process information and make good choices because of health issues. So in my judgment "wisdom" just like "house" or "car" can be taken away from you, so in that sense it a circumstance.

On the other hand we have learned from our experiences and become wiser because of them. In that sense wisdom should be on the quality side of our paper.

I have given you this example in order to show you that in a few cases an item may really belong on both lists. For the most part, however, it should be fairly easy to distinguish between a quality and a circumstance.

<u>Qualities</u>   <u>Circumstances</u>

_____   _____

_____   _____

_____   _____

_____   _____

_____   _____

_____   _____

_____   _____

_____   _____

_____   _____

_____   _____

_____   _____

Now that you have your categories, look back on your original list. Of the first five or six things you thought of, on which side of your second paper did you place them?

Initially most people find it easy to list the things they value: their house, car, job, money, health, and family. After making five or ten entries that end up being classified as circumstances, they start adding qualities like honesty, integrity, and peacemaker as things they value. Isn't it interesting that, like Miss America, I can value world peace, but that is a circumstance? On the other hand being a peacemaker is a quality.

Go back over your categorized list and think through

again how you have each of them listed. Most will be easy but a few you might have to discuss for a while before you agree on where the item is placed.

This is one of the challenges of parenting. As a couple we may not agree all the time about how we want to raise our kids. Parents and partners need to work through the differences and eventually make the choices upon which they agree, choices anchored in the values everyone labels as the most important.

Circumstances are often what we use to measure the success of a life, but circumstances come and go. If I organize my value system around a big house, a fancy car, or other things that can be taken away from me, then I give other people control over that aspect of my life. If my job is the most important thing in my life and I lose my job then I can feel like my life has no value. If money is what I value most in life and I have a bad day on the stock market, I may react like some did in 1929 and commit suicide.

Emotions are often involved with our circumstances and that makes our circumstances even more fleeting because emotions emerge and fade. If we make choices based on emotions we may be like the man who spent his life climbing the corporate ladder only to find out in his later years that his ladder was leaning against the wrong building.

Conversely, if what I value is honesty I do not have to worry about losing that quality in my life. I can give away the quality of honesty by choosing to lie, but it can never be taken away from me. I have total control over the presence of that quality in my life. In the same way if I value kindness I do not have to worry about losing that quality. Some can accuse me of acting without kindness, but since I know what is true, I know whether I had kind intentions or not.

As parents, we choose what we teach our kids to value. To a large degree our children will value what we value. They will learn from us because we will set the pattern for them to follow.

So even through you may not agree on one hundred percent of the items that are on your list, you each need to agree completely about the things you will agree to teach your kids. Together you need to be consistent!

When you and your spouse choose what you are going to emphasize as you raise your kids, use the Four Core Needs as signposts. They will tell you how you are doing in your efforts to raise your kids well. We will discuss meeting the core needs more in Step Five.

For now, remember you and your spouse, or you and your parenting partners, are a team. One may be stronger at giving affection and the other at giving discipline, but it is the parents' and partners' responsibilities as a team to meet the needs represented by your child's four core needs.

One spouse may be stronger meeting one core need, the other spouse more capable of addressing another. How it's done is up to the parents to figure out. Regardless, the child needs their core needs met and it is the parents' job to make it happen. No excuses, no finger pointing. It is not about how one or the other may be doing, it is about how you are doing as a team to meet the core needs of the kid.

In addition, one parent can't give all the discipline and the other dole out all the affection. That is not fair to either parent or the kids. If Dad is a better disciplinarian than Mom, a tendency could exist to let Dad hand out all the negative consequences. Mom might be fond of saying things like, "Just wait till your Dad gets home!" In this example the kids start to fear Dad getting home because no matter when they misbehaved during the day they will get in trouble when he walks through the door. That is not fair to the father or the children. Kids start to see the characteristic of parenting within Dad, like it or not, as being only discipline. They see him as the "bad guy" because he is the enforcer of negative consequences.

This happens in families where Mom may be more caring and empathetic than Dad so there is a tendency to let her pass out all the affection for the kids. Dad might be fond of saying things like, "If you want to read a book go find your mother, I'm too busy." That is not fair to Mom or the kids, either. What is needed here is balance so children don't see Mom as the affection giver who never disciplines or Dad as the only one who disciplines and doesn't offer much affection. What is happening is that the kids start seeing Mom as the one they like and Dad as…well…Dad just isn't liked very much. No matter what our natural tendencies are, we should strive to be more balanced in the way that each parent meets some portion of each child's four core needs.

When the kids' Four Core Needs are met on a consistent basis they can move beyond an immediate need for survival and start to look at how they want to live their lives. This is a sign of maturity. The next step for their growth happens within the Three Cornerstones of Life Is Full of Choices.

Kids cannot realize the differences between qualities and circumstances when they are just trying to get enough affection to meet their own need. They will not notice how their choices affect either their life or other people's lives when they are mainly searching to find someone in their life that can provide boundaries for them. They will not be able to separate what has been done to them from an event they may have caused if they are focused only on their need for someone to be a consistent presence in their life.

Only when their needs for affection, boundaries,

consistency, and discipline are being met can kids look beyond the immediate and see what they can make of their future.

As you meet the four core needs of your kids, you can also take them with you to the top of the mountain. Here they can see where they have been, where they are, and the direction your family is going. Those moments may not have a huge and immediate effect, but as you continue to meet their core needs and choose to take them to the mountaintop day after day eventually they will see the value in the view and want to be there with you. The "value in the view" will feel to them like a deposit in their affection account.

They will help you see how you can be more effective in meeting their core needs. In short, parenting will get easier — not easy, just easier.

Step Two Action:

- Make your list of what you value and categorize the list as qualities or circumstances.
  - o You will learn much about yourselves and what you will end up teaching your kids.
  - o You will learn the process of agreement.
    You will know you have been successful when you have worked together and have these lists and categories on paper.
- Choose from your list the most important things you

want to emphasize as you raise your kids.

- o Talk it over. Most of the time it is not as easy as is sounds.
- o When you have made your choices, mark the ones that are the most important for your kids to value as they become adults.

You will know you have been successful when you have marked some of the values on your list.

- Start deciding how to emphasis those things you most value on your list.
  - o Use the next few pages to make a plan.
  - o Keep track of your successes and less-than-successful moments. Write them down so you can look back at them.

  You will know you are being successful when your vocabulary starts to change to reflect your agreed values.

- Together, work on being consistent in meeting your children's four core needs.
  - o Evaluate where each of your strengths and weaknesses are and work on strengthening your weaker areas.
  - o Take note of the changes that are happening in the choices you make in order to be more consistent, and reward each other as you get more comfortable operating in all four areas of your kids core needs.
  - o Notice and write down how your kid's behaviors

change over the next few weeks as you more consistently meet their needs.

You will know you are successful when you appreciate the value of what your spouse is doing in your kids' lives, and when more time is spent talking about the positive changes than complaining to each other about your kid's negative behaviors.

Journaling Pages for Step Two

As you write this portion of your story pay attention to the processes you have gone through in selecting the things you value as you meet your kid's four core needs. In the years to come you will be especially interested in the answers to these questions:

- What things did you have trouble classifying?
- How are you going to emphasize the things you value the most?
- What have you done to recognize which of the Four Core Needs are the harder ones for you to work in, and what are you doing to improve these "weaker areas?"
- How are your kids reacting to the changes you and your spouse and parenting partners are making?

Journaling Pages for Step Two

Journaling Pages for Step Two

3
Step Three: Change Your Vocabulary

You have found the top of the mountain that works for you. You've had a family meeting where you have explained to your kids the changes that are coming. You have worked through the processes of recognizing the differences between qualities and circumstances. You are now ready for the next step.

Now you must look at your vocabulary. Words are very important—in fact, they're vital. You must find the words that have sent conflicting messages to your kids and erase them from your conversations with them. You must substitute those words with others that better convey the true meaning of what you are trying to say.

Look at the differences between the words *decision* and *choice*. For example, when I talk to people I try to avoid using the word *decision*. When I inadvertently use the word *decision* it causes a red flag to go up in my mind as I am talking. Here's why: a decision is a mental exercise and doesn't necessarily lead to anything. In contrast, a choice has to happen before an action can take place. We never get into trouble for a decision we have made. Trouble can be the consequence, however, if an unwise *choice* has been made.

Another example: a more insidious message is communicated to our children when we talk about life as if it "just happened" without responsibility or cause. When we talk about what we did yesterday it might be normal for us to say something like, "We need to eat toast for breakfast because I didn't get to the store yesterday to buy milk."

That statement, while it sounds completely normal, shows a lack of ownership and responsibility for an action that occurred based on a choice that I made yesterday. It would be better for my kids to hear, "I chose to work in the yard too long yesterday and because of that choice I didn't have enough time to go to the store for milk, so we need to have toast this morning." The result is the same: we need to eat toast, but the ownership of what happened yesterday only shows up in the second example, and the kids start to learn responsible behavior by seeing it unfold.

So a comment like, "On the way home today I got a ticket for going through a red light." would be better expressed as, "On the way home today instead of stopping for the yellow light I chose to speed up to try and make it through, and got caught."

And another: "I gave back the extra dollar the clerk gave me as change today…" could be, "I made the choice to give back the extra…"

In the same way when we hear, "I didn't get my homework done…" we should make sure that the choice is pointed out by saying, "So you chose not to do your homework. During the time you should have been doing your homework, what did you choose to do?"

The process of instilling the importance of choice is best when it starts early in life. When my child kicks the soccer ball in the house I question, "What choice did you just make?" From as early an age as possible I want my kids to take responsibility for their actions. Today it may be kicking the ball. Tomorrow it could be the grade they earn in math class, and in a few years it could be their conversation with a policeman about the candy bar they'd just put in their pocket.

I said it is best to start teaching "choices" at an early age. If your kids are beyond that early age it is still not too late to start. It's never too late. However, the later you start, the longer the process will take and the more work it will be on your part.

When kids realize today that their choice to kick the ball earned them a time out, in a few years when their lower than acceptable math grade comes home it is easier to connect that grade to the choice they made to not do their homework and get it turned in on time. The police aren't interested in why a kid put the candy bar in his pocket. The cop is talking about the action of the kid, not the motive. The juvenile system is full of kids who couldn't connect their action with a possible consequence.

As was stated in *Cornerstones and Core Needs of Growing Kids*: "Dan Wagner, Senior Homicide Prosecutor, Orange County, California commented, 'For several years in my career in the district attorney's office, I worked as a prosecutor of juvenile offenders. In every juvenile offender case, a probation officer prepared a social history concerning the juvenile's family background and upbringing. Reading these reports on a daily basis, I was struck by an unmistakable reality: in almost every case, those youthful offenders had no responsible, caring adult role-model in their life. Not coincidentally, they had an impoverished sense of personal responsibility, no grasp on the consequences of their choices, and no vision for how they could shape their own future. If someone had been building into the lives of those juvenile offenders those kids would not have been breaking the law and getting locked up.'"

As parents we must instill the knowledge that there are differences between decisions and choices. We must teach the practical ramifications that come from making *choices* as opposed to even mentioning decisions. If my kids are going to understand that actions have consequences, "What decision were you thinking about making?" doesn't have the same ownership of action as "What choice did you make?" Parents and partners in parenting, to make a difference in your kids' paradigms of life, choose to talk to your kids about *choices*: theirs *and* yours.

Choose to talk to them all the time about their choices and the natural consequences of them. If you see an action about to take place, ask, "If you make that choice what do you think will happen?" You can use hypothetical situations to consider potential actions and results, "If I choose not to mow the lawn today what do you think will be the result?" Everyone is affected by choices. "If that guy over there puts that box in his pocket what will the police do?" "If the cashier gives me an extra dollar of change what choice do you think I should make?" "What choice will I make?" Talk about *choices* not decisions, and talk about choices all the time.

When negative choices are made, they need to be addressed. Lots of time and energy are spent correcting a kid's mistakes. That is normal. We want to protect them, so when they are climbing on the chair we tell them, "No!" When they walk toward the hot stove we tell them, "No!" As they chase the ball into the street we tell them, "No!" This is what parents do. After the danger has passed we can talk about the choice we saw them almost make, the consequence of that choice, and the affect it might have had on their life, my life, and other people's lives.

Another duty of parenting is to be on watch for the good choices they make. When they make positive choices, make a habit of rewarding them. When they share, notice their action, and tell them you saw what they did. Telling them they did a good job and giving them a hug are rewards for positive choices and uplifting actions.

When she helps a kid up who has fallen on the playground I should tell her "Good job!" When he goes with me to the store and doesn't throw a temper tantrum I should tell him that I noticed and that I like taking him to the store when he behaves. When he says, "please" or "thank you" I should reward him. When she does her job without being asked I should reward her. When I ask them to pick up their toys and they do it without complaining, I should reward them.

When I reward them I counterbalance the effects of the times I have chosen to say, "No!" Any parent knows that *no* is the first word that most kids say probably because they hear it so often. Wouldn't it be a refreshing change if the first words out of a child's mouth were *thank you*? I'm not sure that is possible, but wouldn't it be nice?

Rewarding kids for making good choices is not spoiling them. Spoiling happens when we give them something they did not earn or should not have possession of. Spoiling them is what I am doing when I tell them they can't have dessert and I end up giving it to them anyway. Spoiling them is what we do when we reward them for behavior we don't want to encourage. Spoiling them usually demonstrates a lack of consistency on the part of the parents.

The more noise they make, the more we may want peace and quiet. But the more we give into them because of their noise, the greater reinforcement we provide for their behavior. They conclude that making noise in the middle of a discussion works to their advantage. Noise in general seems to come with kids, right? Noise is not bad, of course, but noise that is made in order to get what a kid wants leads us in the wrong direction. We set the boundary on what is acceptable. From the top of the mountain we choose how much and what type of noise is acceptable, and what to do when that level is exceeded.

Just like the kid in the toy store who is throwing a temper tantrum in the aisle because Mom won't buy him the latest thing-a-ma-jig, throwing a temper tantrum is a fairly normal event for a young child who wants most of what they see and really wants anything they are denied. Usually if the parent will just back away and ignore what is happening the child will realize that their tantrum is not working and will quit.

When a child makes a threat, usually the best course of action is to call their bluff. The child will soon realize they can only hold their breath for so long. Eventually they will quit screaming and at some point they have to eat.

Reward behavior you want to encourage, because the behavior you reward is the behavior you are going to observe over and over again. As you reward their behaviors you are meeting their core need for *affection*. Over time they will reward you by becoming less demanding. Meeting this core need is important to their understanding of what occurs on the mountaintop.

Remember: they don't have a mountaintop view yet. They need to use *yours*, to see *their* future. And even if they were able to climb the mountain and look to the future they wouldn't know how to interpret what they see. So they need you to interpret what they are seeing when you are together on the mountaintop. Take them to where you see what lies in front of them, and explain all that you see to them.

Over time, and I mean over lots of time, they will enjoy hearing you talk about your view of their future. They will begin to believe in what you see. *Repetition* is the key to making this happen and letting it sink in for the long haul.

Sharing what you see from the Top of your Mountain can sound like:

- When I see you sharing your toys I see that you really care for other people. With that attitude you could be a doctor some day.
- When I see you encourage your brother I see that you care about his feelings. With that attitude you could be a teacher some day.
- I saw you put that cookie back in the cookie jar. That shows me that you care about following the rules. With that attitude someday you could be a lawyer, judge, or policeman.

Sharing our views from the top of the mountain gets our kids ready to grow into responsible adults. We want the kids of today, when they become the parents of tomorrow, to find a mountaintop for themselves and raise their kids from a place of peace and contentment.

Step Three Action:

- Look at your vocabulary and choose your words carefully.
  - o Listen for *decision* and eliminate it from your vocabulary. Use *choice* instead.

- o Listen for words like *always* and *never*. Never say never because you will always be wrong.
- o What comes out of your mouth will be a key component of your consistency.

You will know you are being successful when your words more accurately represent what you want to say. As you are more careful in the words you choose there will be fewer hurt feelings and more times of consistent communication, choices, and actions.

- When you use the word *choices* you emphasize the choices that are being made.
  - o Find ways to insert the word *choices* into conversations.
  - o Spend a day and keep track on paper of how many times you use the word *choice*.
  - o Then try to beat your record.
  - o Compete with your spouse to see who can use *choices* the most. Reward the winner!

You will know you are having success when you start hearing your kids use the word *choice* or one of its derivatives.

- Find ways to reward the behavior you want to encourage.
  - o Spend time and energy seeking out moments and methods to reward your kids' positive behaviors.

o Share and compare notes with other people to discover new ways of rewarding positive behavior.

You will know you are being successful when your kids come to you to tell you what they have done that deserves a reward. Words like, "Did you see when I..." are good indicators that they appreciate what you are doing. Answer with, "Yes! I did, and I was so proud of you..." or "No, I was looking the other way. Tell me what you did." Letting them tell you the story is almost as good a reinforcement as the reward you give them. Sometimes let them tell you even if you did see what they did.

Journaling Pages for Step Three

Journal about your choices of vocabulary, how your new vocabulary has impacted your kids, and the results you have enjoyed. Others will be especially interested in the answers to these questions:

- What specific steps did you choose to take to overcome your vocabulary habits?
- How successful have you been in changing your vocabulary?
- What are you doing to reward specific behaviors in your life and in your kid's lives?

Journaling Pages for Step Three

Journaling Pages for Step Three

4
Step Four: Avoid Power Struggles

A power struggle is a test of wills between two people. The person who wins is usually the bigger of the two, the one who yells the loudest, or, most significantly, the one who can endure the longest in the conflict. The main tool of the bigger and the louder person is intimidation. The tool of choice of the one who can hold out the longest is the application of guilt or misdirection by changing the subject.

The secret for an adult to understand power struggles is to realize they are usually events driven by emotions. If I choose to control my emotions, I stay out of a power struggle, and I win. If I choose to let my emotions control me, I will lose. Even if I win this argument, I will have lost the battle with my child because they have been successful in engaging me in a power struggle.

Our culture wants us to react constantly at an emotional level. That's what TV commercials are all about. That is why news reporters who are standing in front of a flooded house ask, "Now that you have lost your home, how are you feeling?" That is why it is standard practice in politics to bring one or two people forward to put a face on the problem and so illustrate how damaging it will be to eliminate this program or that entitlement. The goal is *not* to understand reality; it is to create an *emotional response*.

That mindset has carried over into parenting. If I want my son to put away his toys, I tell him to do it. I say, "Put away your toys. It is time to take a nap."

He responds, "No."

"You have to put away your toys now."

"Why?"

I am being trapped in a test of wills when I say, "Because I said so."

"I'm still playing with them."

"You have to put them away because it is time to take a nap."

"I didn't have to put them away yesterday."

"I know, but today is a new day."

"I don't want to take a nap."

"If you don't take a nap you will be cranky all afternoon and we will both be miserable."

"But I am hungry."

I got sucked into a test of wills when I repeated what I said and felt the need to say, "You have to..." When I repeat a directive I am on the edge of a power struggle or have already entered one. When I reinforce my directive by saying something like, "I said so" or "I'm the boss" or "because it is my house" or my all-time favorite, "because I am bigger than you," at that point I've gone so far over the line that I have to look backward to see where the power struggle started.

When I give a directive the first response most kids will offer is, "No" or "Why." If I engage in a discussion, or even worse an argument with them, I am giving them the mistaken belief that they have the power to question the process. That mistaken belief, when extended into adolescence, teen years, and eventually adulthood produces grief for them, for me, any other authority figure they come into contact with, and all their peers with whom they cannot resolve their personal struggles. This erroneous belief can portend disaster.

Allowing them to control the conversation rewards bad behavior and they come to believe that this is the way to resolve their conflicts. Do not allow yourself to get involved in a power struggle with a child. You are not engaging in a meaningful conversation with a small adult at this moment; he is playing you *and winning* if you allow him to direct the conversation in this way and at this time. It is the back and forth that is so damaging.

Cornerstone Number Two of Life Is Full of Choices says that my choices can affect the circumstances of my life, both now and in the future. If I try to make my son do something, I may succeed; sometimes I'll fail. In the end he feels like his struggle was against me. In this process he sees that sometimes he wins and sometimes he fails but all he has to do is struggle more often against me and by the law of averages he will win more of those battles.

In order to avoid losing even one of those battles all I need to do is change the struggle. I need the struggle to be against the boundaries, not against me. Pick the boundaries that allow you to choose what you want and are willing to consistently enforce. What the boundaries are doesn't matter as much as finding the ones that work for you. Once you are sure that your boundaries are reasonable and age-specific, explain them and enforce them.

Changing the struggle does two things. First, you never lose. You can give up if you choose to, but if you stick to the boundaries and follow the patterns you established when you were on the mountaintop you will never lose a power struggle with your child because you won't be in one.

Second, instead of criticizing, nagging, and fighting you become the child's cheerleader. You become the person who is saying things like:

- It is your choice. What do you want to do?
- I know you will make a good choice.
- What can I do to help?
- Now you have to go to timeout. That is a bummer. I wish you hadn't made that choice.
- Isn't it frustrating when it doesn't go like you thought it would?
- I know how you feel.
- Do you need help making this choice? How can I help?
- I know you will do better next time.

None of those statements are confrontational. In fact they all can be seen as contributors to his affection account. All of those statements empower your child. All of those statements fit into a scenario where you just gave your child the choice of picking up his toys, getting something to eat, and taking a nap.

Revisiting the conversation above, it should have sounded something like this: "It is time to pick up your toys and take a nap."

"No."

"The boundary is that you need to respect me and the stuff, so you have a choice. You can pick up your toys now and we will have lunch before you lay down for your nap, then when you get up we can go to the park for an hour.

"Or, if I pick up your toys, we will have lunch before you lay down for your nap, then when you get up we will clean your bedroom. Which choice do you want to make? You have one minute to choose and start picking up your toys, or I will pick them up and that will be your choice. I am setting the timer right now."

It is hard to tell on the printed page but in this conversation my voice is never raised. I had to think for a minute before I started the conversation because I didn't want it go the wrong way. That would have made it more difficult for me.

In this illustration I broke the processes down into bite-size pieces and explained what was going to happen in little words so everyone involved knew what to expect. I wasn't saying what I wanted to happen — I was telling him that within these boundaries this is what was going to happen, if these boundaries were crossed this would be the result. In fact, I explained that his choice would reveal the result he'd prefer.

If he makes his choice to play at the park, and the timer has beeped, and he has started to pick up his toys, I can help him and say, "I think you made a good choice to go to the park. I really wanted to spend some time playing on the swing with you..." or something equally affirming.

If on the other hand he chose to wait until the timer beeped without making a move to start picking up the toys, I would start to pick up the toys and would say, "Okay, the timer beeped. When you wake up from your nap we will spend some time cleaning your room." The first time this happens, he may at that moment start picking up his toys, but probably not. What is most likely going to happen is he will try and engage you in another power struggle.

If he is not picking up the toys before the timer beeps the choice has been made. If you give in, you teach him to wait it out and see what happens.

"But I don't want to..."or "Wait a minute, I didn't understand..." No matter what is said or occurs following the first beep, if you continue the discussion you choose to lose. If, however, while you pick up the toys it escalates beyond a reasonably disappointing reaction, you can say, "You are not being respectful of me or the toys. I guess I am going to have to put these toys away in the garage for today until you learn how to respect them." At this point you are choosing to place the responsibility of the action onto the child, where it belongs, and the child will begin to understand that the disagreement is with the boundary, not with you.

We are no longer on the power struggle of picking up toys. You have succeeded in staying out of that struggle. Every time, for the rest of the day, that he wants to play with his rolling what-cha-ma-call-it you get to say, "Remember when you chose not to respect me and your toys by not putting them away when I asked, so that I had to pick them up for you? They are now in the garage for four more hours. Let's go look at the clock and figure out when they will come out of the garage and you will get to play with them. You will get that rolling what-cha-ma-call-it back at 6:00 o'clock, which is after dinner. Then you can play with it again. For now, let's go out back and play catch."

Yes, he never picked up his toys. But the power struggle didn't occur, either. Yes, you had to pick up his toys, but he learned a lesson about respecting the toys and the boundary. You may need to do this three or four times, or maybe a hundred times, but at some point *if you are consistent* he will learn that he cannot get away with it, the consequences will begin to work, he will start making different and better choices, and your life will get easier.

It won't all be fixed today or overnight, of course, but today is the best day to plant that seed in his life. It is much better than waiting until he is older and wishing you had done it sooner. Today is the start of a process that will result in his taking responsibility for his actions. That life lesson is a great one for him to learn.

Another good exercise for avoiding power struggles is to start with a question that frames the consequence. For example, "Do you want to put your toys away now and go to the park when you wake up from your nap, or do you want me to pick them up and put them away for the rest of the day and you and I spend some time cleaning up your room after your nap?" A question can be a better starting point that a directive. If you get into the habit of using questions first you can save your orders for special occasions so the orders will have more power. Directives should be saved for when you really need them, like when you see her running with scissors, going into the street to get the ball, or playing with matches.

When Sheryl and I went to language school in preparation for our time in Honduras as missionaries I discovered a very intriguing aspect of the Spanish language. In Spanish, there is a way to conjugate verbs that expresses them as urgent or important without having to raise your voice. The word *stop* in English is what I would yell at a child as he was running into the street to get his ball. In Spanish I could say that corresponding word in a conversational tone and it carries the same urgency as if I screamed it in English.

When I get into the habit of raising my voice to indicate that I am now at the point of taking action, my kids get into the habit of not responding to me in any meaningful way until I raise my voice. The raised voice becomes the call to action. The solution to this dilemma is to never get into the habit of raising your voice.

In a calm, conversational voice you say, "You need to turn the TV down. If you don't do it now I will turn it off and you won't be able to watch TV for the rest of the day." Then when they don't respond to your request, you turn the TV off.

The important part of that paragraph was the last five words of the last sentence, "you turn the TV off." Your actions have to follow your words because you are exercising consistency. The amazing part is that once your kids get used to your calm and conversational voice *and that you do what you say,* they will start responding to you without you feeling the need to raise your voice. This is true because actions speak louder than words. I don't have to yell. My actions just need to be consistent with my words.

Throughout the day as you work with kids you will experience a wide range of emotions. They need to see you happy, sad, expectant, upset, worried, but they don't need to see some of the more damaging emotions directed at them. I can be angry at a choice my child makes without being angry at them. I should be sad when I see them make an unwise choice, but I'm sad at the choice, not them. As the kid's cheerleader I am sad *for* the kid, not sad *at* the kid. I can be mad about the choice without being mad at my child.

When I react with a negative emotion at a choice my child makes, instead of at the child who made the choice, the balance in my child's affection account goes up because I am saying I care about them. For example, when my son is in the backyard playing with a ball and all of a sudden he yells to tell me he is going next door to get the ball, I have a choice about how I am going to react.

If I react at *him* I could be saying, "No. You can't go over there. We'll get the ball later and maybe you will learn your lesson by not being able to play with the ball for the rest of the day. You do this all the time and you need to learn this lesson."

If I choose to react at the *choice* I could be saying, "No. You can't go over there. What is the rule?"

"That I can't go into their yard without permission."

"Okay. Since the ball is over there what are the consequences?"

"I have to wait until someone is home to get permission to go into their yard to get the ball. But I want to play with that ball *now*!"

"I understand, and this is really a bummer, but tell me, who caused the ball to go over the fence?"

"It slipped, so it isn't my fault."

"I am really sad that the ball slipped out of your hand and went over the fence but since you made the choice to throw the ball, and since it ended up over there, now we need to wait until someone comes home."

"But you could go get my ball."

"Yes, I probably could, but then I would be breaking the rules. Is choosing to break the rules a good thing?"

"No."

"Why don't we play another ball game, and when the neighbors come home you can go over and get permission? Then tomorrow I'm sure you will do a better job of not letting the ball slip out of your hand. So right now why don't you go get the…"

In both examples the same information was shared and the same result occurred. The difference is profound: in the first one my son feels like he is being yelled at and in the second example, although a little more time is required, he goes away feeling heard, encouraged, and respected. Plus, I taught him an important lesson that the rules apply to everyone, not just kids.

How about this example? What if say things like, "Why are you throwing the ball?" or, "What are you doing, kicking your sister?" These questions are accusatory and rhetorical. I don't really expect an answer, because there is no good answer.

Instead, if I say, "I'm sorry you chose to throw the ball. What is the rule for throwing the ball?" my son gets to respond. He answers, "Five minutes of time out and I lose the ball for the rest of the day."

My response is, "Give me the ball and I will see you in five minutes."

After I tell him that his five minutes are up then I can say to him,"I'm sorry you chose to throw the ball. What happens if you choose to throw something else?"

"Seven minutes in time out and I lose that toy, too."

"That is right. I know that you will make better choices this afternoon. Now, can I give you a hug?"

The same conversation happens for hitting his sister.
- He tells me what the rules are.
- He goes into time out.
- When time out is done we have a short discussion about why he was in time out and what happens if he chooses to commit another offense on the same rule.
- Then I give him a hug.

Emotions come in three intensities—strong, mild, and weak. Kids watch and learn from us as we experience and express them. Complimentary, positive, and "strong" emotions related to being happy, like excited, overjoyed, and ecstatic, should be aimed *at* them because it builds the kid up. Doing this in abundance encourages them to become a confident and positive child.

These same emotions can be directed at the choices they make. In both cases the balance in their affection account is going to rise. For example, I direct a positive emotion *at* my child when I say:
- I love who you are.
- I love choosing to be with you.
- You are the light of my life.
- I am thrilled to be with you!
- I am excited we have chosen to go to the park.
- I am overjoyed that you are my son!

Directing a positive emotion at the choice that has been made could look like this:

- That is a great choice.
- I am so proud of you for sharing your toy car.
- I just love it when you choose to ask for a hug!

Strong negative emotions like sad, angry, and scared should never be aimed at the child, rather at the choices they made. It is easy to accuse the child of making us feel negatively. It is more productive to talk in terms of the choice and how I feel when I see the choice. For example:

- "You make me sad when you hit your sister..." could look like, "I am sad when you make the choice to hit your sister."
- "You make me so mad at you when you throw food at the ceiling fan..." could be: "I get so mad when you choose to throw food at the ceiling fan."
- "You scare me when you run into the street..." could be expressed as: "It scares me when you choose to run into the street."

Expressing emotions is not bad. How and when we express them determine whether they are uplifting or damaging. Use emotions to your advantage by choosing where you aim them.

I want my kids to see me as the all-knowing, all-powerful, loving, concerned, and caring father I am, not the mean, nasty, grouchy person I could be seen as if I am not careful. I want to be the cheerleader for my kids. I want to be the safe place where they can tell me what is going on in their life without the fear that I will take it out on them. Yes, they will be held accountable, but it is not in either of our best interests for me to belittle them for the choices they make.

When we started talking about parenting in the book *Parenting From the Top of the Mountain* we said, "We should be bringing up kids who have the qualities and skills necessary to become positive and contributing members of society." One way we can do this by taking them to the top of the mountain and showing them the view.

It is easy to get caught up in disciplining negative behavior. I want my kids to act well, so I "train" them, and on a good day they "perform" like good kids. Depending on their age their actions tend to be a result of what they are feeling or how they see themselves at the time. As small children they may want something and reach for it, or they ask for it, or they make a commotion in order to get it. That is normal for smaller children. As they get older we should give glimpses of the big picture so their view of who they are and how they fit into the wider scheme of things is larger than how they feel or what they want.

When they do something good we should respond with positive reinforcement about their choice and an explanation of how that action looks in their future. We can show them a direct connection between good choices and good circumstances.

When we take our kids to the top of the mountain we have to consider what discipline is all about. When we discipline our kids, consequences are given because of behavior. But we need to look beyond their behavior and try to find the motive. Once the motive is discovered we can use both negative consequences and positive reinforcement to shape life's circumstances and create the character we want in our child.

We should not be afraid of using negative consequences. When used consistently, negative consequences are powerful tools to encourage positive character development. They are just as powerful as positive reinforcement and the lessons are more precise. When negative consequences are used in an inconsistent manner, the result is often a frustrated child who exhibits his frustration with anger. The problem is not the negative consequences but our lack of consistency in applying the discipline.

Our goal in discipline should always be character development. It doesn't matter if their choice of behavior produces positive or negative consequences. Both can lead to character development if we look beyond the action, find the motive, and use the opportunity to develop the character we want.

This is difficult to do in the valley because it is normal to get caught up in the behavior, but our goal should be to build their character! Make the choice on the mountaintop to look for character building opportunities.

Our choice of words determines if we are punishing him or building character in him. When little Johnny hits his sister we give him a time out for hitting his sister. That punishment addresses the behavior. When we give him the time out for not respecting other people, we are building character.

So it goes like this:

"Johnny, you hit your sister. What is the rule?"

"I get time out for five minutes."

"That is right. What rule did you break?"

"I hit my sister."

"No. That is what you did, but the rule is, 'Respect other people.' By hitting her you didn't respect her. Take your five minutes of time out and I will talk to you when that is over."

The issue I am dealing with is hitting. Hitting is not good, of course, but talking about not hitting only reinforces the idea that he doesn't want to get caught the next time he feels like doing it. I need to look beyond the act of hitting and deal with the lack of respect for other people.

When he gets out of time out, I take him aside and calmly say to him, "When you hit your sister what qualities are you choosing to have in your life?" Depending on his age he might not be able to tell us, so we tell him that he is becoming mean, vengeful, and nasty and that it makes us sad to see him developing those characteristics in his life. We also can say, "I would rather see you talk to your sister about the problem and work through it with her. That would build qualities of kindness, care and concern for others. I like seeing those qualities in people."

We don't reward behavior we don't want to see again. So I don't spend a lot of time talking to him about behaviors we don't desire. Too much one on one time dealing with behaviors we don't want can be interpreted by a child as a deposit into their affection core needs account. Therefore, we discourage the behavior we don't want with a quick reminder of what we do want. In all cases we constantly strive to build our relationship with the child!

While doing this we are emotionally on the top of the mountain. We are not yelling. It's a quiet conversation, pointing him toward his future, showing him what happens if he keeps making a negative choice. We do this not because he will never hit his sister again, but to build in him the pattern of looking at the future through our eyes so he can see what we see for him. To the child this is framing his life so he sees where he is going, where he will end up, and what is going to happen to him along the way.

He wants our approval. When he shares the ball with his sister, we need to reward him instantly. Then, when we are praying with him before bedtime we can remind him of what he did and talk about the positive qualities he is developing in his life — those of kindness, compassion, and empathy. We can talk about how proud we are of him for being kind to his sister. "You know what? Since you were so kind to your sister tomorrow morning I am going to make my special pancakes for breakfast." Remember: we reward behaviors we want to encourage.

Through the emotional ups and downs we all experience, rest assured that mistakes will be made and parents are not immune from making them. Parenting is about the end result, however, not about every moment of time spent getting there. As you look at the day you will see moments you would like to do over again. We all do this. Don't choose to beat yourself up over the moments you slipped off the mountaintop. Apologize for errors and head back up to the mountaintop. Tomorrow we will try to avoid the booby traps that exploded in our faces today. If we focus on today, when tomorrow comes we will most likely repeat what we did today. If we focus on the booby traps, those traps are where our emotions will take us. So, we apologize and move on.

I'm sure there was a cowboy who said, "You need to get back on the horse." The same is true in parenting. You need to get back on the path that you intended to be on, the path that will take you where you want to go.

Start like this. "I'm sorry I yelled today when you took the knife out of the dishwasher. I should have remembered it was in there and taken it out before I asked you to empty the silverware. I just got really scared when I saw that knife. I was scared you were going to hurt yourself. Will you forgive me?"

"Mom, I forgot all about that."

"I am glad, but I want you to know that I am sorry. Will you forgive me?"

"Sure I will."

"Thank you. Tomorrow we are going to have fun. Now sleep well and I will see you in the morning."

As we spend time learning how to parent from the top of the mountain we may have many moments to apologize for. Don't worry about them and don't make a long list of *mea culpa* explanations. This is not about us. It's about our kids. We are teaching them that no one is perfect, that at times everyone needs to apologize. We are teaching them how to apologize and how to recognize when an apology is needed by doing it ourselves.

Choose a couple of moments you would like to do over, and model for your kids how to apologize. Over time you will develop more skill at keeping your feet firmly planted on the mountaintop and your apologies will be fewer. As the need for apologies lessens, it doesn't make them any less important. When we apologize from the heart we are teaching our kids how to be positive and contributing members of society.

No matter if we have something to apologize for or not, we end every day with a hug and a kiss. Remember, it's about the kids.

Step Four Action:

- Avoid power struggles.
  - o Practice with your spouse on how the power struggle game is played. One of you try to start a power struggle, the other one try to avoid it. Take turns trying to avoid the power struggle.
  - o Learn that once you have made the choice to get into a power struggle the best thing you can do is to walk away. After you cool down you can come back and start over again.
  - o Practice starting with a question instead of a directive.

You will know you are achieving success when you can see the power struggle developing and you choose to stop. The short version is, "When you are in a hole, stop digging."

- Become a cheerleader when negative consequences are required.
  - o Look for ways to encourage.
  - o Remember you are not the bad guy. The choice of the child has caused this. The child actually is choosing to have a time out.
  - o Choose to direct your emotion at the choice and its consequence rather than at your child.
  - o Your joy is when you tell your child, "Next time you can make a better choice."

  You will know that you are successful when it starts to feel natural to take your kid's side against the consequence. It is you and her against the world.

- Never raise your voice except in an emergency.
  - o Keep track of what is happening when you start raising your voice. Compare notes with your spouse to find out if you have a pattern. Work on breaking a negative pattern.
  - o Remember: emotions are good. Choose when and how you will use them. Use emotions to your advantage. Don't get caught up in your kid's emotions. Stick to your plan.

  You will know that you're becoming successful when you can go through half a day without losing your cool. You are even more successful when you set your sights on a whole day, then a week. Your goal is to consistently use emotions to your advantage in raising good kids.

- Apologize when needed. In the beginning you will not be as consistent as you would like to be, so you will need to apologize.
    - o Practice with your spouse. Learn how to be sincere.
    - o Learn how to apologize, not make excuses or give explanation.

    You will know you are being successful when you feel better after apologizing.

Journaling Pages for Step Four

As you write this portion of your story you may want to make notes to remind yourself how using emotions to your advantage is paying off. Others may be helped by the answers to these questions:

- What are the power struggles in which you've found yourself and how are you avoiding them?
- How are you rewarding the positive actions of your kids?
- When is it most difficult to control your emotions?
- What has worked for you as you have tried using your emotions to your advantage?
- What results are you seeing in your kids' lives as you have been using emotions to your advantage?

Journaling Pages for Step Four

Journaling Pages for Step Four

5
Step Five: Meet Their Four Core Needs — Use the Three Cornerstones

The Four Core Needs

Affection
Anything we do to make a child feel good
about him or herself.

Boundaries
The pre-arranged limits that are placed on behavior.

Consistency
Doing what you said you would do.

Discipline
The actions that are taken to instill in a child
the understanding of right and wrong
in order to shape their character
so they learn how to make healthy choices.

The Three Cornerstones

Cornerstone Number One — Empowerment
Life is full of choices,
and the choices I make today
will determine the qualities of my life
both now and in the future.

Cornerstone Number Two — Responsibility
Life is full of choices,
and the choices I make today
can affect
the circumstances of my life and
other people's lives
both now and in the future.

Cornerstone Number Three — Freedom
Life is full of choices,
and even though I have not chosen
all the circumstances of my life,
I alone determine its qualities, because
life is full of choices,
and the choices I make today
will determine the qualities of my life
both now and in the future.

The Four Core Needs are tools that help parents interpret our kids' actions. When they are yelling in the house, you deal with the yelling, then try and figure out which core need that yelling manifested. Are they asking for *affection*? Is your *consistency* in question? Do they need to be reminded that the *boundaries* are still in place? Can you calm them with a small dose of *discipline*?

As you evaluate their emotional needs and take steps to meet those needs, they will be comforted. Part of that comfort will come from your concern for them. The bigger part of comfort will come when you actually figure out which core need is deficient and make a deposit into that core need account.

Remember that they are telling you what their need is; they are just doing it in code. Look beyond the action in order to break the code.

Their actions give clues to determine which of the four core needs accounts currently has a void and how that void can best be filled. Instinctively the kids know which one it is, they are just not good at knowing how to ask. If what they need is affection and you provide discipline, their need goes unmet and they will keep asking for affection in ways that can be disruptive to the household, the family, and your peace of mind.

At the second meeting of a two-session parenting seminar one mother shared that she started using the Four Core Needs after the conclusion of the first session a week earlier. Her four year old, Julia, would get up from her afternoon nap and be stomping around the house. She was obviously upset and her mom had had no clue what to do other than send her to her room until she calmed down. Since she understood the four core needs she asked her daughter if she wanted some "hug time." Julia just sat for about ten minutes on Mom's lap. Even though other things were going on around them, they took the time to share some affection. The next day after naptime was over Julia started stomping again. Mom was busy and it went on for quite a while. Finally Julia came up to Mom and said, "Mom, can I have some hug time?"

Now that Julia knows what to ask for when she is in a stomping mood her knowledge will make tomorrow, and many tomorrows, easier. It is important, therefore, that parents know their kids. Beyond that, it is important that parents and parenting partners are willing to look at their parenting habits and evaluate what they are doing and how that looks to the kids.

As parents, everything you do with them, for them, and to them will affect the balance in at least one of their four core needs accounts. Your actions affect those accounts either positively or negatively. Once you meet their emotional core needs they can move beyond felt needs and deal with other larger issues. These may consist of questions like these:
- Who am I?
- What do I want out of life?
- How can I contribute to society?

As long as they are focused on getting their four core needs met they are incapable of looking at those bigger issues.

First and foremost, meet their core needs.

- Pass out *affection* like it is candy on Halloween.
- Choose and thoroughly explain the *boundaries* you will be using.
- Use *consistency* as the measure of your success.
- Follow your *discipline* plan to build character.

Don't get sidetracked by thinking about what you cannot do for them. If it's not possible to buy that new gadget that everyone else has, remember that the gadget is a circumstance. Go back and review the list you created in Step Two that showed you the areas of life where you want to have the most impact, whether in circumstances or qualities.

The goal of parenting is to develop good qualities. As you work on qualities you will be building character. Character will determine if you have been successful in raising good kids.

Use your understanding of your kids four core needs to meet their immediate needs. They will tell you by their actions when they have a need. Knowing the categories of need helps you figure out what their current need is.

After you have met their Four Core Needs on a regular basis the Three Cornerstones of Life Is Full of Choices are used to point their attention to their future.

The first cornerstone is the first one because it is the most important of the three, not because it is the easiest place to start. Understand that when you use the Three Cornerstones the second one will make the most sense to your child. If you start with the first cornerstone and repeat that over and over again until "they get it" you will grow tired — it doesn't work. Kids will understand how their choices will affect their circumstances easier than comprehending how qualities matter. Once they understand how their choices affect their circumstances, however, it is an easy step for them to understand that what applies to circumstances also applies to qualities.

Until now we have looked at these cornerstones and focused on how they help your kids look to the future. Now begin to see how these cornerstones can *empower* you as you view your *responsibility* with *freedom* from the guilt of unrealistic emotional expectations.

It is difficult for some parents to hear and understand this, at least at first. Your kids will make both positive and negative choices. There nothing you can do to change that. When they choose to hit someone you can affect their circumstances with consequences but you cannot change the character their choices produced. If you spend your time and energy trying to change their character, you are trying to accomplish something in an area over which you have no power; you are wasting your time. Instead, spend your time and energy passing out affection, creating boundaries and consequences, and working toward consistency in your interactions as you discipline them.

The choices your kids make will shape their circumstances when you consistently enforce the consequences. You can have an affect in this area. But remember, your boundaries and consequences can only affect *their* circumstances. You cannot control their life or their choices — you can only affect their circumstances.

Your kids will make choices that will affect the circumstances of other people's lives. The older they get, the more this is true. And the older they get the less you can affect their circumstances. When they are infants you have quite a bit of control. Enjoy it while you have it. In a few years you will have less, and by the time they are school age, you will have even less.

Multiple examples in movies and commercials tell us that we tend to see our kids as kids even when they have grown up. The good news is they are not babies forever; the bad news is once they start growing up, that process accelerates until one day we look back and wonder, "Where did my child go?" They go from the child who needed his pants pulled up to a young man who wears the pants in his own family.

Somewhere in this process parents should realize that in three areas their kids grow to become independent. These areas are emotional, physical, and financial.
- They no longer rely on their parents for their emotional well being. They get a good portion of the deposits they need in their affection account from someone

113

else. Of course, that is good. They have become an emotional adult.

- When they become a physical adult they usually exhibit this by moving out of your house. They choose to do that for a feeling of independence from Dad and Mom. That is good, too.
- A financially responsible adult demonstrates independence by not needing money from you anymore.

Congratulations, you have done your job. There is no more parenting to be done. You have done it all.

You are still a parent, or a parenting partner. If you are the parent, that infant you carried will always be your child. When they become an adult your advice will be sought out on their terms, not yours. This is harder for some than it is for others but it's always a rude awakening for every parent to know that the relationship with their child has changed. As a parent my presence may be wanted but not needed. I may be asked my opinion, but I am no longer the key voice in making things happen.

The relationship I established at the beginning of their life will determine the parameters of how and when my adult kids *may* seek me out.

- Because I helped them realize the importance of qualities over circumstances and taught them how their actions affect other people's lives they will eventually thank me for that gift by caring for me as a person.

- Because I taught them that what happens to them is not as important as what happens in them, they will ask for and sometimes treasure my advice and my company.
- Because I instructed them in the truth of Cornerstone Number One I will find freedom for myself knowing that I am not accountable for their qualities.
- Because I taught them the truth in Cornerstone Number Two I will find freedom for myself knowing I am not responsible for the results of their choices in their lives or the lives of others.
- Because I educated them in the truth of Cornerstone Number Three I will find freedom for myself in the knowledge that it is possible for them to find their own healing for the traumas caused by life.

When you know and choose to accept what is important in life, you can use the three cornerstones to focus your efforts and let the rest go.

Step Five Action:

- Practice looking beyond their actions to see their needs.
    - o Study your kids and develop a sense of what their needs are. Each spouse should listen to each other as you do this. You will both have good insight.

o Identify and write out a child's most needful area. This area will change over time but at this point it is the most important one on which you want to focus.

o Focus on meeting that Core Need.

o Pay attention to how meeting that core need affects their perception of the world and their place in it.

You will know that you are being successful when their attitude starts to change. They will be happier, more content, and easier to manage.

- Meet their need.

o Review all four of the core needs in the order of their importance to your child. As you meet their need in a new area don't forget about the core need you were just successful in addressing. Focus first on just one, then two, then three, and finally you will be able to consistently meet all four of their core needs.

You will know you are being successful when their attitude continues to improve. They will not be "out of control" as much, and when they are a little wild, a little "hug time" or something else, depending on their current core need, will take care of their issue.

- Practice using The Three Cornerstones as a calming influence in your life.

o Keep the Three Cornerstones in front of you. Put them on the refrigerator, paint them on the wall, hang them in a picture frame, and stick them to your bathroom mirror. Memorize them.

o Say them over and over again to yourself and your kids. As situations arise, bring the cornerstones into your conversation.

You will know you are achieving success when your kids start complaining that you are talking about the cornerstones too much.

Journaling Pages for Step Five

As you write this portion of your story you may want to make notes about how understanding the Four Core Needs of your kids helped you understand your kids' actions. Also record what happened as you repeated the Three Cornerstones to your kids and to yourself. Others may be helped by the answers to these questions:

- How were you able to identify the core needs accounts in which a deposit was needed as you observed a specific action?
- What happened to their attitude as you met that core need?
- How has their attitude changed as you addressed additional core needs?
- What have been the results in your family?
- How has using the Three Cornerstones affected you?

Journaling Pages for Step Five

Journaling Pages for Step Five

6
Step Six: Reward, Reward, Reward

This step is so basic I hesitated to even make it a step to the top of the mountain. However, as I reflected on my own life and many conversations with parents, I came to realize that in the busyness of life this basic step often gets overlooked. There have been times when I have overlooked it.

Blinking is important to the health of your eyes but we hardly ever think of the need to blink. Breathing is important to the health of your body but we hardly ever think of the need to breathe. In the same ways, positive reinforcement is critical to the well being of the relationship we are establishing with our kids. The difference between blinking and breathing, and positive reinforcement is this: we need to *remember* to use positive reinforcement.

Again, reward behaviors you want to encourage. When the kids do something good, notice it. Make a list of what you and your spouse or parenting partners consider to be "good choices." Figure out how you want the kids to behave, what you want to see more of, and get serious about rewarding those choices.

- Tell them you noticed.
- Let them hear you telling other people you noticed.
- Tell them you told other people you noticed.
- Tell them how other people felt about what they did.
- Write notes to them.
- Make certificates to put on their wall.
- Create a chart to keep track of times when they "made a good choice."
- Tell them when they are being punished that you remember when they did something good.
- Embarrass them by announcing to their friends that you noticed. (They will complain that you do this, but they will secretly like it and their friends will all wish they had someone saying those things about them.)

This is not rocket science. This is common sense.

If my boss yells at me every day at work, pretty soon I will dread going to work. If every time I drive by a policeman I get a ticket pretty soon I will turn whenever I see a police car on the street. If every time I go to the doctor I get a shot, pretty soon I won't want to see the doctor.

When your kids do something you don't like, correct the behavior. But spend far more time on reinforcing positive behavior. When you spend time offering positive reinforcement the kids take positive attributes away. What they take from the positive processes are feelings like this: "I get to spend quality time talking with Mom (or Dad). I'm going to remember this for the next time I feel the need for some alone time with them." Most of the time that is not a conscious thought. It is a feeling.

One on one time with Mom or Dad is a great reward. The problem is that in our busy lifestyles, many kids don't get enough of that quality time, regardless. Worse yet, some parents both work so their kids have to be in day care and the time with Mom or Dad, or a parenting partner, is even less.

Use of day care is making the best out of a bad situation, but it can be done. Parents and partners are better than a paid substitute, of course, but if you have to have your kids in someone else's care, find someone who will treat them like they are their own.

We have a very close friend who takes care of other people's children. Her name is Glenna. She provides day care in her home. Glenna does an excellent job of taking care of "her" kids. She limits herself to a very small number of kids. She is well organized about the things they do. Her facility has good rules and the kids all work to make it a great place to be.

I have spent time in her home and I have seen the joy in her kids' eyes as they see her in the morning.

Glenna is so positive about her kids. She spends time everyday affirming their individual strengths and encouraging them to be great. The kids want to be with Glenna because their core needs are being met.

If you have to use dare care, find someone like Glenna to take care of your kids. They will be happier and better behaved when they are at home, and you will know that they are getting what they need when they are away from home.

Because quality time with parents is hard to come by anyway, parents who withhold quality time from their kids as a consequence of children's poor choices compound the problem of children not getting enough of it to begin with—a lose, lose proposition. I don't have a problem disciplining a child for crossing a boundary as long as in the process I show him I love him. But I do have a huge problem when I hear about parents who get so upset when their child spills a glass of water on the floor that they will not comfort the child with a hug.

Meeting the core need of affection is not a reward for your child. Affection is one of his core needs that must be met, regardless. Affection should not have to be earned. It should be given, and given, and given some more. There are no boundaries on affection! Meet this core need in any and every way you can, and when he is in trouble give him more.

There are times when our emotions get in the way of feeling like we can give affection to our kids. I heard a story once where a kid put a cat in the dryer and turned it on. I would have a problem feeling affectionate after that, but in the middle of the consequence there needs to be a hug anyway.

Whenever consequences were given to our kids I tried to have a conversation with them that went something like this:

"Do you know I still love you?"

"No." (Or they can answer "yes;" either one will work.)

"I do. I'm disappointed with the choice you made, but I still love you."

In whatever situation you find yourself you should make sure your affection is consistent. Again, affection knows no boundaries.

Rewards for good behavior should show you care in ways beyond satisfying immediate wants. If you give food as a reward, make it healthy food, not candy. If you give money as a reward, make sure part of it goes into savings for college and part of it goes in the church offering plate on Sunday morning. Remember, you are establishing patterns they will take with them through life. However you choose to reward your kids make sure you are rewarding behavior you want to encourage.

Step Six Action:

- Each of you, make a list of ways to reward your kids then compare the lists.
    - o Ask your kids how they want to be rewarded.
    - o Talk to other parents to get new ideas.
    - o Pick two or three of the best ones to use this week.

    You will know you are being successful when you can see in your kids faces that they are enjoying life more than before.
- Keep track of the ways you have rewarded your kids for a week.
    - o How has their behavior changed?
    - o If it has not gotten better, change your rewards.
    - o If it has gotten better, do the exact same things for another week but add another type of reward to what is already working.
    - o Talk about what is working every night with your spouse.

    You will know you are successful when they smile just to see you coming.

Journaling Pages for Step Six

Add stories to your journal about the reward systems you are using, especially about what the kids say when they are rewarded. As you tell your story to other parents they may want the answers to these questions:

- What first steps did you take to reward your kids?
- How did their behaviors change that first week?
- What rewards have worked over time?
- What rewards have not worked?
- How has rewarding positive behaviors changed their outlook on life?
- How has rewarding good behavior changed your outlook on parenting?

Journaling Pages for Step Six

Journaling Pages for Step Six

7

Step Seven: Be Consistent

In *Cornerstones and Core Needs of Growing Kids* we defined *consistency* as "doing what you said you would do." I also said, "Trust is built on consistency. I can't trust someone who is not consistent. Broken promises produce disenchantment, distrust, and resentment.

"Consistency is hard work. In fact, acting with consistency becomes the hardest part of working with children. Achieving consistency is even harder when you are working with a staff! The simple truth is this: as hard as it is, the efforts are worth the results. The rewards of consistency are worth the commitment!

"Consistency was the only tool I had (yes, the only tool)

that made disciplining children at the Community Center easier and effective. In groups made up of children and adults, if the adults weren't willing to regularly enforce the boundaries, children would push hard to find out what they could get away with. Allowed to continue the kids would eventually take control and the result would be chaos.

"Someone was always in charge at the Community Center. Leadership abhors a vacuum. Either the adults would control or the children would. Consistency was the key to establishing who was in charge. When I or another adult was running things our kids learned how to act within the boundaries that we established.

"Actions speak louder than words."

In order to be consistent, if you say it, you must do it. Therefore, don't say it unless you can do it. As parents we expect our kids to trust us. The trust of a child is given to their parents almost from birth, but that trust can be lost. With enough broken promises a child will harden his heart and quit trusting his parents.

Being consistent requires that you are aware of what you are saying. Say what you mean, mean what you say.

"I'll do that when I get home."

"You're going to get it when we get home."

"We can go on that vacation next summer."

"When you are _____ I will buy you a _____."

"If you ever do that again, I will _____"

All of these statements are perceived by your child as contractual obligations. They came out of your mouth so now you are committed to making them happen. The child doesn't care that you are tired when you get home, or that on the way home you started to feel guilty for what you said, or that the stock market collapsed and you can't afford that vacation. As you fill in the blanks of life, he doesn't care what they are, he only cares that you are consistent.

Your consistency will determine his self worth.
- If you follow through on what you say you will do he will feel like he is important to you.
- If you do not follow through on what you say you will do he will feel like you don't care about him.

In the waiting room of my doctor's office I watched a mother and her very active five year old girl. I heard the mother say, "Sit here and don't you get up..." at least a dozen times. I heard her say, "Come here right now!" more times than I cared to count. I heard her say, "Don't do that again." time and time again as the child repeated her same behavior.

I thought of so many stories I could tell, but what really got my attention was when after the daughter slid off the bench seat for the umpteenth time the mother grabbed her daughter by the arm, pulled her close and with a great deal of anger in her voice said, "All right, when we see the doctor I am going to ask him to give you two shots." I've never known doctors to give shots as a punishment for misbehaving. I think it might be a conflict with their Hippocratic Oath. I am certain, however, that the mother has some serious challenges in her future with respect to the behavior of her daughter. When the little girl hits adolescence there is no telling what that adolescent teenage girl will do based upon a history of doing whatever she wanted to do and getting away with it.

I was leaving a grocery store. Right on front of me was a mom, and a girl who I thought to be eleven or twelve years old. As we were walking I heard the mom say, "If you are going to act like that, I will never bring you to the store again."

Now that was an interesting statement. I am intrigued by definitive statements, especially when they contain words like *always* and *never*. *Never* is a long time! The girl said something like, "Mom, everyone has those for lunch; I just wanted to try one." When I heard the daughter say *everyone* I figured out where the definitive statements came from. This was getting interesting. Mom replied, "I don't care what everyone else is doing, when I say 'No' I mean no, and I don't like it when you throw a fit in the store."

The girl had been drinking out of a can. She finished it right then and chose to throw it down in what I can only describe as disgust. Mom burst forth, "Now you listen to me, young lady. You go pick up that can and throw it in the garbage right now!" The girl kept walking toward the street and her mom kept up the verbal tirade. The volume was going up with every step. Mom exploded, "Don't you dare walk away from me. Go back there and pick up that can. Don't make me get mad at you. I will only tell you one more time. You are going to be in so much trouble when we get home."

Eventually, even with ever increasing volumes, the voices faded. I only hope that someday this mom might realize that she was fighting losing battles. She was engaged in power struggles she couldn't win. She showed a great lack of consistency, and the boundaries were unclear. Worse yet, whether she knew it or not, she was going to lose the war over the behavior of her daughter.

At the beginning of this section I quoted a statement I made about the Community Center in which I talked about consistency being even harder when you are working with other staff. You may have said "This is a parenting book. Why is he talking about staff?"

You and your spouse are the staff of your "youth program." Your baby sitter is part of the staff, too, and if you are lucky enough to have grandparents involved in your kids' lives, at some point, they will be staff as well. The truth is that over the years there will be many people who will have a hand in raising your kids. There probably will be many partners in parenting.

The process will go more smoothly if all of the staff members follow the same rules. Working together is even more important when we are talking about you and your spouse, the primary care givers. Babysitters can be forgiven because they are not a permanent fixture in your child's life. And grandparents, well, as a grandparent, I can say for certain that we have a tendency to do what we want. We can be difficult to control. That's okay, though. For the most part babysitters and grandparents come in and out of a child's life. Kids have the ability to realize that since they come and go, the differences in meeting their core needs and enforcing discipline don't matter as much as they do for parents. Dad and Mom however are always there. What they do, or don't do, matters.

If you want to effectively parent using the rules and tools of *Seven Steps to the Top of the Mountain*, the people who are raising a child need to speak with one voice. This is another example of consistency. When a child comes to Mom and receives an answer, the child needs to know that if he goes to Dad, the answer will be the same. If he doesn't like Mom's answer and thinks he can get a better one from Dad, he will continue to play one of you against the other until you resolve this inequity. Your child is in a no-lose situation.

If Mom says "No" and Dad says "Yes" the child learns that all he has to do is say, "Dad said I could." If Mom and Dad start arguing about who was right and who was wrong, the kid is home free because now the parents are mad at each other and the next time he wants something he will go to dad first.

If the parents get mad but don't argue, the kid will probably not get in trouble (whew!) because each parent is wondering what the other wants to do. If the parents go into the other room to try and work it out, the child gets to watch some more TV. Whatever punishment may come his way will come later, not now, and for him that feels like a win. For him, it is a win. Besides, at this point he knows that he can get away with playing one parent against the other. He will just save that gimmick in his bag of tricks for later.

Consistency is reacting to the same stimulus the same way, day after day. Consistency is two people responding as one person, day after day. Consistency is speaking with one voice.

Consistency is hard. As an individual you will make mistakes. That's normal. You as a couple will make mistakes. That's normal, too. That is why we learn how to apologize and get back on the track of being consistent.

We have already looked at how and when to apologize.

You may want to review Step Four: Avoid Power Struggles (page 79). An apology from you starts the process of your child rebuilding his trust in you. Without an apology, you have broken trust and that trust will never be completely rebuilt. Apologizing for mistakes is a part of being consistent.

Consistency for the child must be present in the words and deeds from all the caregivers who make up "your staff." Without consistency you have disconnect, broken relationships, and unreasonable and unrealized expectations. Without consistency you have adults going through the motions of being parents, but not parenting well. Without consistency you have kids who want to take control and usually do. Inconsistency results in turf battles, and unwinnable wars. Inconsistency is a poor choice.

Conversely, when consistency is present you have agreed standards, order, and peace. Consistency is your key to meeting the Four Core Needs of your kids. Consistency is still the key when you are using The Three Cornerstones to help them grow into responsible healthy adults. Consistency is what parenting all about as shown in *Parenting From the Top of the Mountain* and *Seven Steps to the Top of the Mountain*.

Step Seven Action:

- While you and your spouse are at the top of the mountain do an honest evaluation of how consistent you are as a couple. This is not a time to go back to saying things like, "You were not consistent when you…" or, "I always see you…" or, "Whenever he does _____ you always give in." Remember, you are a team and you are building upon what you agree.

- o Discuss when you are most consistent.
- o Ask if there are certain situations that cause you to be inconsistent.
- o Have some kind and loving conversations about what is happening at the moment we become less consistent.
- o Keep score for a week of the times you are less consistent than you want to be.

- Re-enter the process and do another honest evaluation of how consistent you are as a couple.
  - o Follow all of the points that you covered in the first evaluation. Be honest in your assessment. Celebrate your wins and keep working to correct your losses.
  - o Keep doing this loop until you see some success in being consistent. This is hard work; it may take quite a bit of time! Don't give up.

  You will know you are becoming successful when you can each share about your inconsistencies and work together to become more consistent.

- Encourage each other as you make improvements in your consistency.
  - o Spend time and energy doing this. Remember "reward behavior you want to encourage" works on adults too.

o Don't rush the process.

You will know you are being successful when you can share how your day went and laugh about your inconsistencies with each other.

- Ask each other, "How can I let you know when I perceive you are not being consistent?"
    - o Agree on the words to use or a signal you can use.
    - o Go through another week trying this signal on your spouse when it is needed.
    - o Talk about it and change the signal if needed.

    You will know you are being successful when you can each use the word or the signal without the other person getting mad or defensive.

- Go back to the list of boundaries you created for your kid's behaviors and work on being consistent with them, again.
    - o Talk it through and find the boundaries that will be the most difficult.
    - o Develop your plan with specific steps to help you with the difficult boundaries.

    You will know you are becoming successful when you can look back on the week and see that the steps helped you in some specific situations.

- Make a list of how you as a couple are improving your consistency.
    - o This list will encourage you to do better. You will see that the hard work is starting to pay off.

- o Celebrate your successes.

  You will know that you are being successful when you celebrate regularly.
- Make a list of how your consistency is evident in your kid's behavior.
  - o This is one of the rewards for behavior that needs to be encouraged in your children.
  - o This is one of the ways to reward yourself. When they change their behaviors as a result of the choices you have made, that is a good thing.
  - o Rejoice!

  You will know you are being successful when you can point to specific times your kids have exhibited behavior that is not consistent with previous behavior. They have changed!
- Go back to the list of boundaries you have created to define your kids behavior, and work on them again. Setting boundaries is a never ending process for parenting from the top of the mountain.
  - o Find new boundaries with which you are having problems.
  - o Establish replacement boundaries.
  - o Evaluate the boundaries all the time, to make sure they are good.

  You will know you are successful when you are excited about becoming more consistent.

Journaling Pages for Step Seven

Consistency is hard. Other parents who hear your story of striving for consistency may be encouraged by hearing the answers to these questions:

- How difficult was it for you to become more consistent?
- In what area was it the most difficult?
- What worked for you to eventually become more consistent?
- How did you signal each other?
- What milestones did you see as you traveled toward consistency?
- What are the pitfalls others should avoid?
- What changes have you seen in the behavior of your kids as you have become more consistent?

Journaling Pages for Step Seven

Journaling Pages for Step Seven

Conclusion:
Starting All Over Again

Parenting is never over as long as you have kids at home. If you have kids for whom you are responsible you will always be actively engaged in meeting their needs for affection, boundaries, consistency and discipline. Just when you think you have it all mastered, your grade school child becomes an adolescent and it will seem like everything that used to work went right out the window as the hormones kick in.

Parenting is a struggle as you strive to stay one step ahead of them as they grow into that next stage. If you have two or three kids it will seem like someone is going into a different stage every day. That is not true, but it will seem like it. What worked for one kid will not work for another. You will need to design new boundaries and consequences that work for each child.

When we sent Brian to his room as the consequence for doing things we didn't like, we were not accomplishing our goal of applying a needed consequence for wrong behavior. It took us a while to realize that for him, being sent to his room was a reward, not a punishment. Paul, on the other hand, hated to be left alone. A time out for Paul was the perfect consequence for negative behavior. Find what works for each of your kids. Be consistent and stick with it until it doesn't work. Then be quick to change to something else that does.

Parenting is hard, but you can do it well if you:
- Start from the Top of the Mountain.
- Plan where you want to go.
- Have a target, a landmark, to aim at.
- No matter where you are physically, emotionally stay focused on the view you had from the top of the mountain.
- Meet your children's Four Core Needs.
- Imprint on them The Three Cornerstones.
- Be consistent in what you choose to do.
- Physically return to your spot on Top of the Mountain. Go there often. Parenting is better from there.

Acknowledgements

Creative Team Publishing (CTP), www.CreativeTeam Publishing.com, has been great to work with. Glen Aubrey, Deanna Christiansen, and Jordan Trementozzi have provided creative writing and editing processes. It is great to work with an organization that understands what you are trying to say and then makes suggestions that help get you to the destination you desired in the first place.

Finally, even though you can't judge a book by its cover, a book without an attractive cover is just a government report. A good cover attracts our attention. It encourages us to pick it up and take a look. Justin Aubrey has exceeded the expectations I may have had. He has created the three book covers in the *Life is Full of Choices Series*. I like them all, but I love the one he designed for *Seven Steps to the Top of the Mountain*. It is my hope that you get as much out of the books as all these people have put into them.

Some years ago Sheryl chose to get a Masters Degree from Fuller Theological Seminary in Intercultural Studies. While she was thinking about it I said that I would help her in any way I could. While she was taking classes she would often come to me with the idea for a paper she was writing. She knew the material and many times had pages and pages written but she would say, "It just doesn't feel right. Can you help me?"

We would talk and talk and I would read what she had and eventually I would make a few little suggestions that would move one thought in front of another one and change this paragraph so it accented the idea she was trying to convey.

I came to enjoy the times of taking ideas and reorganizing her thoughts into a coherent pattern that would allow them to make more sense. Over the years something must have worked, because as a result of what I did to help, or in spite of what I did, she earned her degree.

That practice helped me in the process of writing this book. I have taken the truths of *Parenting From the Top of the Mountain* and condensed them into seven manageable steps. Thanks, Sheryl, for the time you spent with me helping me practice a skill I didn't know I would need.

The "Choice/Destiny" ambigram was hand drawn by world renowned ambigram artist, Mark Palmer. Mark is the owner/artist behind Red Chapter Clothing, a premium line of clothing and accessories based entirely on his unique ambigram artwork. If you are interested in seeing more, go to our web site and follow the links to Red Chapter Clothing.

When Sheryl and I chose to become missionaries, the first seminar our mission provided for us was two weeks of media training. They helped us learn how to tell our story. They also taught us the mechanism of what to do when you have an hour's worth of story to tell but you're given only twenty minutes in which to tell it. This book started out at thirty-seven steps to the top of the mountain. We can all be grateful for this missions training.

In writing a book on parenting I need to emphasize again the effect my parents have had on me. As I was growing up I can't begin to count the number of times they said "No." and "Don't do that." But I can't ever remember them saying to me, "You are not capable of doing that." When I wanted to play a better guitar than the one I got through the catalogue for $14.99 they found a way for me to earn the money to buy the one I wanted. When I wanted to get a job, they didn't buy me a car, but made it possible for me to use one of their cars, arranging their schedule so I could take my mom to work before I had to be at school. I don't think they ever said, "Life is full of choices." They just lived it in front of me every day.

For most of the past 31 years Sheryl and I have been working together. At one time while Sheryl was going to school she didn't work at the Los Angeles Community Center, but most of our time in ministry has been spent working as a team. Most of that time, I was in charge. I had the title of Director and led the staff we worked with. The exception was a few years that we were on staff with Campus Crusade for Christ where Sheryl had a position in the HR department. During those years she enjoyed being my boss.

When something needed to get done we never worried about who had the title or whose job it was supposed to be. We just did what we had to do to get the job done. The successes we enjoyed in the lives of the people with whom we worked can be directly attributed to the willingness we had to work together to get the job done.

While these books have my name on the cover as the author, they would not have been possible without Sheryl's care, encouragement, and not a few swift kicks. I appreciated the support, enjoyed the encouragement, and have realized that occasionally I needed the kicks.

Thank you, Sheryl, for these books which really are "our" books.

Life Is Full of Choices
www.LifeIsFullOfChoices.org

life is full of choices

What We Believe:

Life Is Full of Choices is an organization that believes people have the power to choose the qualities of their life. When people choose their qualities they determine who they are and how they will be perceived by those around them. We believe qualities of life are more important than any circumstances.

What We Do:

We teach adults how to work with kids. Adults create

lasting impressions on these young lives as they pass important qualities from one generation to the next. We show them effective methods of training kids to make better choices.

We also teach kids. It's fun, challenging, exhausting, and rewarding. We learn from them as we teach them. In fact, they are some of our greatest instructors.

Why We Do It:

Remember, it's about the kids. We have the responsibility to train them about choices, consequences, empowerment, responsibility, and freedom. Join us as we help kids today and positively affect lives for their generation and many to come.

John and Sheryl Emra
Are Available To Speak
To Your Group

Please visit www.LifeIsFullOfChoices.org.
Contact them about scheduling a Life Is Full of Choices
event for your church or with your group.
schedule@LifeIsFullOfChoices.org

For individual mentoring:
mentoring@LifeIsFullOfChoices.org

Contact John and Sheryl Emra by phone.

(855) AT LIFOC or (855) 285-4362

Purchase "choice" products at
www.LifeIsFullOfChoices.com.